EMERGENCY COMMUNICATION 101

Adams Media
An Imprint of Simon & Schuster, LLC
100 Technology Center Drive
Stoughton, MA 02072

First Adams Media trade paperback edition November 2025

Interior design by Sylvia McArdle
Images © Adobe Stock; 123RF
Photograph on page 143 © Getty Images

Manufactured in the United States of America

1 2025

Library of Congress Control Number: 2025940331

ISBN 978-1-5072-2445-8
ISBN 978-1-5072-2446-5 (ebook)

EMERGENCY COMMUNICATION 101

THE ESSENTIAL GUIDE TO Maintaining Contact During and after Any Disaster Scenario

CREEK STEWART & JOE BASSETT

ADAMS MEDIA
NEW YORK AMSTERDAM/ANTWERP LONDON TORONTO
SYDNEY/MELBOURNE NEW DELHI

CONTENTS

INTRODUCTION

In terms of surviving during and after a disaster scenario, communication is critical. However, the uncomfortable truth is that the normal communication systems we rely on for our daily life activities are in fact fragile infrastructures that are prone to damage and disruption. Whether it's getting in touch with loved ones, reaching out to first responders, securing resources, or receiving in-bound disaster–related updates, the ability to communicate in times of emergency can make the difference between life and death. In an emergency, you simply can't afford to be offline or out of touch.

In *Emergency Communication 101*, you will learn how to create a personalized emergency communication plan for you and your family. You'll be equipped with the knowledge, tools, and resources to effectively communicate with emergency responders, family members, neighbors, and others even when the normal modes of communication are unavailable. In this book, you will discover:

- The vulnerabilities in the modern communication grid.
- What radio services and setups are available and most applicable for you to use.
- How to set up an emergency communication go-kit.
- How to power your communication tools at home, on the road, and in the field when the electrical grid has been compromised.
- What radios, tools, and services are available to receive disaster updates and information.

- Basic radio etiquette and operation.
- What your options are in the satellite communication space.
- How to create a comprehensive Family Communication Plan that can be deployed in the event of a disaster.
- And more!

Communication is critical to establishing goals, making decisions, developing strategies, and executing plans during a disaster scenario, but often people overlook the entire category of emergency communication. *Emergency Communication 101* will help you gain clarity on what steps to take, what gear to purchase, what skills to know, what licenses to obtain, and what plans to make. This comprehensive guide can be the catalyst for an entire mindset shift from being fearful to becoming a confident leader.

If your goal is to learn how to create a reliable emergency communication plan, how to choose the right tools, and how to adapt to various crisis scenarios with confidence, this book will offer you a clear, actionable approach. With it, you can provide reassurance, guidance, organization, and leadership for an individual, a family, or team in the midst of chaos. By the end, you'll feel confident and in control, knowing that you can maintain communication and keep in contact with your loved ones no matter what happens. Remember, it's not IF but WHEN!

PART 1

WHEN THE COMMUNICATION GRID GOES DOWN

The "normal" communication grid is composed of several components that you depend on during any given day. These include landline phones, cell phones, Internet service, radio and television broadcasts, and electricity. Unfortunately, you're just one cell tower, one power outage, one cable, one software glitch, or one major disaster away from being disconnected from one or all of these services.

This is why a backup "off-grid" form of communication is so important. Off-grid communication is any tool or collection of tools that allows you to send and/or receive communication when the normal operation of these services is interrupted. Off-grid communication systems ensure that you can still communicate with families and emergency responders in the midst of a crisis.

Chapters 1 and 2 will highlight modern vulnerabilities and what scenarios can cause communication grid failures, including physical damage, power outages, cyberattacks, and operational overwhelm. Dozens of events can cause either one or all of these to occur, including winter storms, civil unrest, terrorist attacks, rolling blackouts, wildfires, and more. Understanding why systems fail is foundational to developing an effective plan to replace them.

Finally, Chapter 3 will introduce you to a variety of off-grid power solutions. Many disasters interrupt the electricity grid and you must have systems in place for powering the tools you will choose. With the information in these first chapters, you will be able to grasp the importance of the resources and plans outlined throughout the rest of the book.

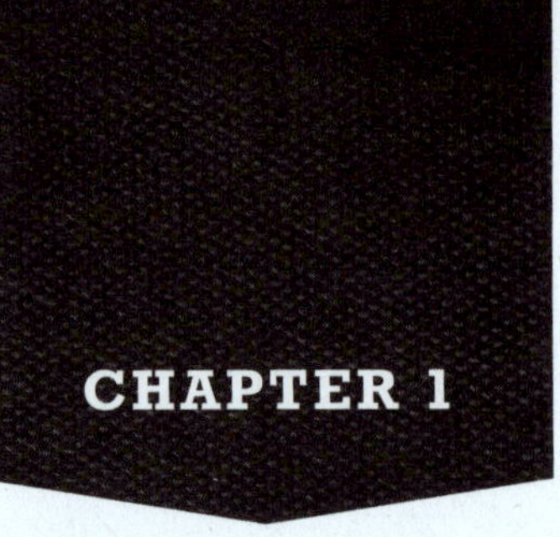

COMMUNICATION SYSTEMS FAILURE SCENARIOS

Before deciding on your alternative communication options and power, it's important to understand what can lead to a communication breakdown. The better you understand the cause, the better you can prepare a solution. This chapter will cover the four most common reasons why modern communications fail. It's important to understand these reasons so that you can make better decisions about the plan you create, the tools you choose, the skills you learn, and the actions you'll take.

There is no black-and-white solution to emergency communication. A thorough understanding of why communication systems fail directly impacts your upcoming decisions. As you read through this chapter, think about the disasters you've experienced and ask yourself which of the following failures you've witnessed in your area before. These are the ones that will likely happen again.

Puerto Rico after Hurricane Maria devastated the island. This physical damage certainly interrupted the local communication grid.

Causes of Communication Failures

While new, unexpected, and unforeseen scenarios can happen at any given moment and interrupt normal communication systems, there are four scenarios that are most likely. Knowing these four causes will help you identify personal vulnerabilities and make plans accordingly. These causes include physical damage, power outages, cyberattacks, and operational overwhelm.

Physical Damage

The most obvious cause of communication system failure is physical damage to communication infrastructure from either natural disasters, human-made disasters, or even terrorist attacks.

Natural disasters of all varieties can cause temporary or long-lasting physical damage to communication cables, cell towers, and Internet services. Nearly every region in North America is affected by natural disasters, which can interrupt communication systems and hardware. Winter storms in the north, hurricanes and tsunamis along the coasts, tornadoes in the central states, wildfires on the West Coast, and flooding along waterways are all responsible for temporary loss of normal communications in the past.

In addition, physical damage can be caused by human-made disasters such as explosions, nuclear meltdowns, acts of war, and terrorist attacks. Just like in the case of natural disasters, repairing or rerouting communication systems after a human-made disaster can take days to months. For example, in March 2024, submarine communication cables were "cut" by terrorists, which affected nearly 25 percent of Internet traffic between Asia, Europe, and the Middle East. Repair of the cable took months due to permitting restrictions.

The severity of physical damage can vary greatly. It can be as simple as a tree branch knocking down an Internet cable to one home or as complex as a hurricane damaging multiple aspects of the communication grid over an entire region. Without backup communication plans and tools, individuals have very little control or recourse when these events occur and are at the mercy of communication operators repair crews.

When assessing how physical damage could affect you and your loved ones, consider these questions:

- What disasters have caused physical damage in your area in the past? These are indicators of what may cause future communication failures. Everyone's local risk is different based on where they live.
- How long will you need to provide your own power and communications? Physical damage requires repair. Depending on the scale of the disaster, repair can take days to months.

Off-grid communication tools are often the only tools that work in events with widespread physical damage. Subsequent chapters will discuss different options for you to consider.

Power Outages

"Normal" communication systems are all dependent on electricity. The power grid is equally as fragile as communication hardware and can be affected by all of the same previously mentioned events. Understanding this connection can help you plan for time when power and communications are both affected simultaneously. Even if communication hardware, switches, or cables are not physically affected, the hardware that enables the creation or delivery of electricity can be damaged. This can include electric poles, substations, electric lines, and dozens of other hardware-related items. Here are a few events from recent history that can help add context:

- In 2011, a 5.8 magnitude earthquake took the North Anna Nuclear Power Station in Virginia offline for nearly ten weeks. This exposed vulnerability and weakness in one of the United States's largest generators and transporters of power.
- In 2013, an organized sniper attack on the Metcalf substation in California did significant damage and exposed how vulnerable these substations are to domestic or foreign terrorist attacks. In just a few minutes with a handful of high-powered rifles, an entire substation became inoperable, and all power had to be rerouted through various generators.
- In 1998, ice accumulation of several inches during winter storms throughout Canada and the Northeast United States caused dozens of electrical poles to collapse. Full recovery from this storm took weeks.

Besides these specific instances, millions of people lose power for undetermined periods of time each year due to countless incidents, including but not limited to winter storms, floods, windstorms, and overuse blackouts. Chances are you can remember the last time your own power was knocked out due to a natural or human-made disaster.

What's even more interesting is that some power outages aren't directly caused by disasters. In 2019, California experienced a record-breaking loss of cell phone and Internet service during the Kincade wildfire. This loss wasn't caused directly by the fire. Instead, the power company shut down power to widespread parts of the state to prevent ignition from power lines and other electrical equipment that were damaged by the high Diablo winds. Even fire stations in the affected areas were forced to communicate solely by radio. This left thousands of California residents without cell service and Internet service. Consequently, residents who did not have backup communication tools or plans couldn't communicate with loved ones or receive information about the wildfire. Regardless of whether the decision to shut down power was good or bad, it is yet another reality when it comes to loss of power. When someone else is in charge of the power, it can be removed.

The bottom line: Power outages due to physical damages can be caused by a number of circumstances, both natural and human-made. While best efforts are being made on all levels, the power grid is very susceptible to interruption the moment things go sideways.

In terms of how power outages can affect you, consider these points:

- Power outages almost always impact the local communication grid.
- Do you have backup power in place to keep your communication tools online or to power your off-grid communication devices? (Chapter 3 will explore numerous off-grid power options.)
- Even when power is available, overuse of regular communication networks (both Internet and cellular) dramatically impacts a region's ability to communicate normally.
- Without a plan to provide your own power, no communications will work, even if you have off-grid backups.

Cyberattacks

Cyber-related attacks pose significant threats to the modern communication grid. These attacks and many others like them continue to reveal the fragility of the communication grid and the software that controls it. Cyberattacks are a modern form of piracy—hijacking unsuspecting communication systems for the purpose of doing harm. From government agencies to private businesses, recent history is littered with dozens of successful distributed denial-of-service (DDoS), ransomware, and other types of cyber infiltration and manipulation.

In addition to economic disruption and access to personal data, entire systems have been affected by cyberattacks, from shipping to communications.

Cyberattacks are the Wild West of modern warfare and the tactics are changing as fast as the technology itself.

With all normal modes of communication now on a digital computer and software backbone, everything from Internet service to cell phones are susceptible to disruption. In 2024, the Chinese espionage group known as Salt Typhoon successfully targeted several large communication companies in the US, including AT&T, Verizon, and T-Mobile. While the Federal Communications Commission has enacted enhanced security measures, it is yet another example of how fast the technology landscape changes.

In terms of cyberattacks, you should consider that:

- Your communication network can be impacted even when everything seems normal and there is no obvious natural or human-made disaster.
- Communication grids are popular targets due to their disruptive nature. Shutting down communications affects many other areas of society. This is a trend that will only get worse.
- You have absolutely no control over many modern communication infrastructures such as cloud-based servers and online messenger programs. Modern communication platforms leave you entirely helpless when the software or infrastructure is compromised.
- Do you have off-grid communication tools such as two-way analog radios that are not connected or dependent on modern service providers? (Chapter 5 will discuss options for this.)

Operational Overwhelm

What's the first thing people do when disaster strikes? They make calls on their cell phones, send texts, and get on the Internet to see what's happening. Just as there is a limited number of first responders to go around in the beginning stages of disasters, the same is true for cell phone and Internet capacity. All of our systems—medical, food production, communications, etc.—are designed for "normal" use. These surges of use during a disaster will cause clogging and failure, at least temporarily, due to overwhelm. This happens even if there is no physical damage or loss of power.

Some points to consider about operational overwhelm:

- Historically, text messages are more reliable in situations of operational overwhelm than phone calls.
- Off-grid communication tools such as ham radios are not affected by operational overwhelm on cellular or Internet platforms.
- The faster you can execute a communication plan before congestion sets in, the more likely your messaging will reach family, friends, and neighbors. (You will outline an executable plan in Chapter 10.)

Quick Action Checklist

As you've learned, failure can come from physical damage, power outages, cyberattacks, and even operational overwhelm. Recognizing these causes is the first step in preparing a plan that can help to navigate them. Using the information provided in this chapter, it's time to assess the likelihood of certain communication failures in your area.

- Identify the top natural disasters that could happen in your area.
- Determine the most likely physical threats to the communications grid in your area.
- Estimate how long you could be without power or communications if physical damage were to occur.
- Make a list of cyber-dependent communication tools you currently rely on.
- Start a communications threat log to track communications failures and their impact in your area.

CHAPTER 2

VULNERABILITIES IN MODERN COMMUNICATION SYSTEMS

As convenient and impressive as modern communication devices are, the grid they operate on is fragile and more interconnected and interdependent than ever. While advances in communications have helped us stay more connected, they have also made the "normal" communication grid more susceptible to disruption by exposing a variety of vulnerabilities. Unfortunately, these exposures are magnified during a disaster. In this chapter, you'll learn about hidden weaknesses built into the modern communication grid, from centralized and cloud-based infrastructure to Internet and power dependence. Understanding these threats will not only help you construct a more modern communication plan; it will help you create one that is more resilient as well.

To build a reliable strategy, you must fully understand where your current communication options will likely fail. Your goal is to make a backup communication plan that is both modern and resilient. This requires a keen understanding of your current communication weaknesses. This chapter will shine a light on some of these areas to help you hone your communication plan.

Centralized Communication Hub

The old "copper wire" landline telephone systems may not have allowed mobile communication, but they were not susceptible to many of the vulnerabilities (such as cyberattacks) of modern software-based systems. In general, it was only damage to the physical infrastructure (such as telephone wires and poles) that disrupted communications. Typically, this was in a very localized area.

But now, vast regions of communications are controlled by centralized hubs consisting of cell towers, fiber-optic cables, satellite stations, and data centers, all which are heavily dependent on electricity and other interconnected systems. Each of these communication hubs have their own set of vulnerabilities; the failure of any one of them can affect an entire region of customers. By recognizing how centralization leads to fragility, you'll better understand the importance of diversifying your communication options with localized and even independent solutions.

For example, cell towers are susceptible to extreme weather, such as ice and wind. They are also susceptible to terrorist attacks, as they are often located in remote areas with little to no security. Data centers have their own unique vulnerabilities; this became evident in 2022, when the United Kingdom experienced a record heat wave. As a result, Google and Oracle's data centers in London overheated and suffered cooling system failures. Both companies had to go offline to prevent further damage.

Besides physical damage, loss of power, and cyberattacks, there is an added issue to these modern systems—overuse. These systems can only handle so much data load. When that load is reached along any one of the connected infrastructures, the system becomes "clogged." The result is sluggish connectivity or loss of communication altogether. This is often seen in times of disaster when too many people from a specific region are trying to call or text on their cell phones at the same time.

In addition, an incredible number of telecommunication professionals are needed to keep these systems operational. According to the World Economic Forum, four million technology professionals are needed to bridge the gap in the cybersecurity industry alone. It takes a lot of trained and skilled individuals to operate the thousands of interconnected cell towers, fiber-optic cables, satellite stations, and data centers.

Dependence on Internet Communication

As if the digital age doesn't present enough problems during disasters, the world is now almost as reliant on forms of Internet communication as it is on electricity. Virginia Tech computer scientist Ali Butt describes what's happening to online communication, specifically the consolidation of infrastructure, best:

"This is akin to replacing all local streets with a highway, where a single crash can shut down the highway, leaving users few alternate options."

Over the years, the infrastructure that enables online communication, such as email, apps, and data storage, has been consolidated to a smaller number of cloud service providers. This magnifies the impact if these centers are affected by physical damage, loss of electricity, cyberattacks, terrorist attacks, or something else. The implications of these outages are further reaching than just disrupting social media and email. Nearly every industry and service, from energy and healthcare to transportation and payment processing, relies on these various systems being online 365-24-7 and functioning properly.

The bottom line is that, if a disaster of any kind disrupts online communication, it will create a second indirect layer of damage on top of the obvious direct damage. Essentially, the vulnerabilities in modern communication systems create an environment where one disaster becomes many, almost instantaneously.

What does this information mean for you? Consider these points:

- It is important to assess which of the services you use on a regular basis will not work when Internet or cellular service is unavailable. You may be surprised to find out how grid and cloud-tied you really are.
- You should make a short-term goal to have at least one form of two-way communication that does not rely on the Internet. The ideal options are either ham or GMRS two-way radios. Upcoming chapters will discuss both of these options.
- It is now very common for important documents and access to important information (and even money) to be dependent on Internet access. It is therefore essential to have physical backups, documented account numbers, and more in case of an emergency. (You'll have an opportunity to

plan this while creating your physical copy of your Family Communication Plan in Chapter 10.)

The Dependence on Electricity

It used to be, with analog landline phones, that one could talk on the non-electric rotary phone during a complete power outage as long as the phone company still had electricity to send power through the phone lines. But now everything is dependent on electricity. On a macro scale, cell towers, fiber-optic cables, satellite stations, and data centers all require electricity. On a micro scale, cordless phones, laptops, computers, routers, cell phones, ham radios, and two-way radios will all require batteries or charging eventually. All modern-day communication tools and the systems that run them will require power, either through the traditional power grid or a backup of some kind.

This creates a double layer of dependency on modern systems. Communication tools are no longer enough. One must also have access to electricity. One is just as important as the other.

In terms of your electrical needs, consider these points:

- All communication tools need power—both on and off-grid. You will need backup power options to have a complete disaster communication plan.
- There are many things to consider when it comes to power and electricity, including portability, renewable sources, fuel, and cost. All of these will factor into your upcoming power strategy.
- You should have a tiered power plan that provides several power options. This will be described in Chapter 3.

Recent Disasters with Personal Perspective

While the following historical lessons may feel beyond the scope for many who just want to set up a disaster communication plan for their family or neighborhood, they help provide a context for the developments of electronic communication in real-world events over the past several decades. While you may never "deploy" to help set up disaster communications, you may very well be put in a position to set up something similar on a smaller scale for your own team, family, or neighborhood. The following lessons from real-world events can be invaluable in your own communications journey, regardless of the scale.

It's easy to think of historical events as "something that happened to other people." But studying historical events provides valuable insight into decisions you can make today. They show you what worked, what didn't, and how you might be better prepared for what will happen next.

HURRICANE KATRINA (2005)

- **What happened:** Widespread flooding caused communication infrastructure failures, especially in New Orleans. Overwhelmed circuits and power failures at relay points caused this communications failure.
- **Lesson learned:** Cellular networks and landline communication are susceptible to congestion and power failure.
- **How this applies to you:** You should prepare alternate communication methods powered by battery, solar, and generators.

In the early morning hours of August 29, 2005, Hurricane Katrina slammed into the coast of Louisiana, Mississippi, and Alabama. Later that day, several people found themselves stranded on a rooftop in New Orleans.

Someone in this group attempted to call 911, but the circuits were overwhelmed. Then they tried calling a relative in a nearby city spared from the devastation. To everyone's relief, the call was answered, but now they struggled to find what could be done from 80 miles away. The relative called the local Red Cross office, which had a ham radio station and operator. He used the radio to contact members of the Salvation Army Team Emergency Radio Network (SATERN), who were actively listening for distress calls from areas in the disaster zone. Two SATERN members, one in Oregon and one in Arizona, answered the call and relayed the information via radio back to a ham radio operator in proximity to first responders in Louisiana, and the group was rescued.

Katrina was an unusual mix of intensity and widespread destruction. The Mississippi coast experienced the fiercest winds, damaging most cell towers and other exposed equipment. Flooding caused significant damage to communication power infrastructure stretching from New Orleans east to Florida and north to Jackson, Mississippi, and Birmingham, Alabama. The combination of all three factors took New Orleans and the Gulfport-Biloxi metropolitan area completely "off the air" and caused sporadic communication outages across hundreds of miles.

HURRICANE MARIA (2017)

- **What happened:** Hurricane Maria devastated the island of Puerto Rico. This knocked out nearly all phone service (cell and landline), Internet access, and first responder radio service across the island. These failures cascaded and repeated over several weeks and months.
- **Lesson learned:** Entire regions and remote communities can be left isolated for long periods. Varied terrain makes short- and long-distance communication very challenging in these instances.
- **How this applies to you:** You should develop a scalable communication plan that accounts for varied terrain and short- and long-distance communication.

Hurricane Maria was the deadliest tropical cyclone of 2017. On September 20 of that year, Maria struck the southeast corner of Puerto Rico, near Yabucoa, and carved a northwesterly swath of destruction across the entire island before exiting near Arecibo. Category 4 winds, as high as 155 miles per hour, heavy rain, and storm surge impacted virtually every structure in its path. Power, communication, transportation, and vital services were out of commission, not just for local communities but all 3.2 million people on the island. Some estimates state that all but five cell towers were damaged. As of this writing, Puerto Rico still suffers from random, frequent power outages.

A few days later, Joe (one of the authors of this book) and several other ham radio operators landed at Luis Muñoz Marín International Airport in San Juan. We were part of the ARRL Force of Fifty, deployed to provide communication support for the American Red Cross (ARC) relief efforts. Our original mission was to collect information from individuals and families who wanted to let their loved ones and friends outside of Puerto Rico know they were safe and well.

A few hours after we landed in San Juan, we met with Oscar Resto. He was the ARRL section manager for Puerto Rico at that time. Oscar had already been hard at work leading ham radio relief efforts. It took him three hours after Maria had passed to clear fallen trees from his driveway just so that he could set up a ham radio station and help direct relief work. Through broken English, Oscar said, "I know you're here to send safe-and-well messages, but the island is desperate. Nobody is safe and well! What Puerto Ricans need is for fire stations, police stations, and hospitals to be able to talk to each other and rescue people." This type of radio communication is referred to as "tactical traffic." As opposed to health-and-welfare traffic, which is written down and can take hours or days to get to its destination, tactical messages are short, concise, actionable messages. The request-response-resolution cycle of tactical messages is measured in minutes.

Joe in the radio room at the temporary Red Cross Headquarters in San Juan. From this radio room, he coordinated ham radio communication between the field operators, the American Red Cross, and the local FEMA office at the Puerto Rico Convention Center.

Unfortunately, our radio antennas would operate best at 20 meters above the ground, but it was nearly impossible to find structures that were tall enough to mount an antenna in a place that was just leveled by 150 mile-per-hour winds. The best we could hope for was 5–10 meters high. Thankfully, setting our antennas at 2 meters high was perfect, with some minor modifications, for a type of radio propagation called Near Vertical Incidence Skywave (NVIS). NVIS signals travel almost straight up a few hundred miles where the ionosphere bends them back toward Earth. Think of holding a water hose vertically so that the water flow goes straight up before gravity brings it almost straight down. NVIS radio coverage usually covers an area within 500 miles of the antenna. That's near-perfect for getting a signal up and over mountains on a 110-mile-long island. So, by simply lowering our antennas, we were able to communicate from one end of the island to the other and most points in between.

By the time we left Puerto Rico three weeks later, robust forms of communication were coming back online. I'd be remiss not to commend the exceptional, selfless work the local Puerto Rican hams did to rescue their island. Their tenacity, resourcefulness, and hospitality carried me through some overwhelming days and nights. Our success as a team wasn't possible without Oscar, his son Ozzie, and the hams of Puerto Rico.

The value of civilians in real-time tactical communication would come to fruition seven years later in 2024 when Hurricane Helene obliterated large portions of the Southeast United States.

HURRICANE HELENE (2024)

- **What happened:** Hurricane Helene's high winds and torrential rains devastated remote areas that generally aren't affected by hurricanes. Vast swaths of transportation and communication infrastructure were wiped out. Relief and recovery efforts were delayed or nonexistent for weeks and months. Self-reliant, well-trained, and prepared civilians filled the communication gaps for an extended period.

- **Lesson learned:** An unexpected disaster will happen and catch the "official" response off guard. Many factors will delay help coming, and self-reliance will be crucial.
- **How this applies to you:** Join or establish a self-supported communication community now. Develop, refine, and practice an actionable communication plan. Be ready to implement it when disaster strikes.

Helene was the deadliest Atlantic hurricane since Maria and the deadliest to hit the US mainland since Katrina. Helene was like two disasters in one. It made landfall with 140 mile-per-hour winds in the Big Bend region of Florida. It weakened rapidly before dumping record rainfalls on the southern Appalachian Mountains. Large portions of the Black Mountain region in North Carolina were devastated by floods.

The mountainous terrain made relief efforts difficult. Large sections of mountain roads were washed away, and in a strange juxtaposition of primitive and modern transportation, some areas were only accessible by pack mule or helicopter. There were also reports of local, state, and federal failures to get help to where it was needed. Whether recovery efforts were hampered by geography or bureaucracy, it can be agreed that government relief efforts were ragged at best.

Despite all these failures, residents rose to the challenge. There are hundreds of stories about neighbors helping neighbors, average citizens sharing resources, and clever people improvising solutions. In addition, local ham radio operators called in rescue workers, coordinated emergency requests, and shared valuable information with the outside world.

Points to Consider

Knowing about these disasters, the devastation they caused, and how they impacted communication in these areas, consider these questions:

- What if this same event happened to your region today? How might your current communication options be impacted?
- What communication tools would you use if your normal options, such as cell phone and Internet, were inoperable?

- Do you have a strategy in place for communicating with friends or family members who may be separated during such an event?

Ongoing Lessons

A hurricane is a unique disaster in that people can plan ahead for a specific time and area of impact. Most other disasters, such as earthquakes, tornadoes, and wildfires, pounce on you without warning. However, the lessons we learn from the "slow-motion" disaster of a hurricane can help us prepare for a "quick strike" disaster like an earthquake.

From Katrina, we learned that total failure of a system is rare. Just because communication is down in one direction doesn't mean it's down in all directions. The people on the roof in New Orleans couldn't get to 911 from where they were, but they could get there from Oregon and Arizona. Luckily for them, they found the other way by accident. You don't have to be lucky. You can use your experience to prepare multiple ways to get messages to where you need them. In Katrina, portable cell service also came online within days of landfall. This reduced the need for long-term health-and-welfare traffic traditionally sent by amateur radio operators.

At the same time, the growth of cell phones and smart devices overwhelms communication infrastructure in the first seventy-two hours after a disaster strikes. Local ham radio operators have started to fill the gap. In Maria, we saw an increased reliance on amateur radio operators for tactical communication. Amateurs tend to be more nimble, adaptable, and resourceful than their professional counterparts. This isn't intended to deride professional disaster professionals. The nature of amateur radio as a hobby lends itself to "making do" with scarce resources. This isn't to say that tactical communication is new to ham radio. The Radio Amateur Civil Emergency Service (RACES) has provided contingency communication for first responders for decades, but tactical communication played a more significant role during Maria.

In the aftermath of Hurricane Helene, amateur radio communicators took matters into their own hands. Even as the rains were still falling in the Carolinas, ham radio, citizen band, and general mobile radio service enthusiasts activated nets and shared valuable and, in some cases, life-saving information through radio.

A bias toward action is a double-edged sword, however. When well-intentioned, ill-informed, untrained, and ill-equipped nonlocal amateur radio operators self-deploy, they risk adding stress to areas already overwhelmed with displaced individuals. They arrive intending to help without an invitation but aren't prepared to support themselves in an austere environment. They quickly become a burden on an already overstressed system.

Finally, throughout these three hurricanes, we see amateur radio operators accept new roles beyond being radio users. Before Hurricane Katrina, there was one widely used wired technology, the telephone, and one dependable, widespread wireless communication technology: radio. If phone service was interrupted, radio was the only substantial backup. The advent and growth of the Internet, cell phones, Wi-Fi, and satellite devices have challenged radio's reign as the king of disaster communication. Successful amateur radio operators master multiple means of communication.

Quick Action Checklist

This chapter uncovered critical weaknesses in the modern communication grid—many of which people don't even know exist until it is too late. From Internet and power dependence to cloud-based infrastructures, each one adds a new layer of risk. Following is a quick self-assessment checklist that will shed light on where you currently stand regarding dependency on modern infrastructure. The more boxes you check, the more dependent you are. If you check five or more boxes, then it's good you are reading this book. Regardless, don't be discouraged. The goal of this book is to "uncheck" as many of these boxes as possible for you.

How dependent are you on the modern communication grid?

- ❑ My primary form of communication relies on my cell phone and/or an Internet connection.
- ❑ If my cell phone stops working and Internet service is unavailable, I do not have a backup communication tool to use.
- ❑ The communication apps I use on a regular basis such as email, iMessage, WhatsApp, and more are cloud-based.
- ❑ I do not currently own off-grid communication tools such as two-way radios or satellite messengers.
- ❑ I do not currently own off-grid navigation tools such as offline maps or physical maps.
- ❑ I do not have backup power options to charge my communication tools in the event of a power outage.
- ❑ I have not tested to see if my communication tools and regularly used apps operate without Wi-Fi or a cellular data Internet connection.
- ❑ I have not created a Family Communication Plan to execute in the event of a communication grid failure.
- ❑ I would not know how to get in touch with my family or close friends if a disaster struck today and knocked out the communication grid.

CHAPTER 3

EMERGENCY POWER SOLUTIONS

All your communication tools will require electricity. Even those that are battery operated will eventually require power to recharge them. Unfortunately, electricity is one of the first services to be affected in a disaster. In this chapter, you'll learn how to build an affordable and scalable tiered power plan. Whether it's a quick blackout or a long-term power outage, each tier is designed to help you maintain power for your critical communication devices and tools.

Building Your Backup Power Plan

For an apartment dweller or a homeowner, losing power can mean some or all of the following: loss of heat, light, refrigeration, hot water or even water itself, communications, Internet connection, Wi-Fi, ability to run medical equipment, and ability to charge devices, as well as stalled sump pumps, inactive sewage grinder pumps, and more.

On a macro level, entire infrastructures can be affected. These include city communications, water pumps, transportation, retail businesses, grocery stores, gas stations, ATMs, banks, restaurants, and delivery services. Food spoilage and water contamination start immediately. Medical facilities and nursing homes will have to rely on backup power, if available, to run critical medical equipment. After Hurricane Katrina ravaged areas of Mississippi, Louisiana,

Alabama, and Florida, it took an average of six weeks before the power in all affected areas was restored. That's a month and a half without electricity!

For most people, setting up a long-term backup power supply, such as a fully integrated solar charging system, isn't practical or in their budget. However, there are several options worth considering that can provide short-term power and/or intermittent power for powering and/or charging critical systems. The more expensive and complicated something is, the least likely someone will do it. Thus, the goal of this chapter will be to offer affordable and easy-to-implement backup and off-grid power solutions that are achievable for the average household.

An emergency communication plan that does not include backup or alternative power is simply incomplete. The advantage of implementing a backup off-grid power solution to run communication tools is that it can also be used to power and charge other devices such as flashlights, laptops, household appliances, water pumps, hot plates, and even power tools.

It is best to think of your backup power plan in tiers. Each tier builds upon the next and provides clear actionable steps to take depending on your goals and available time, money, and resources. A tiered power plan can also help you to scale your response to power loss depending on the particular circumstances. We will start the discussion of these tiers with the least expensive and easiest to implement category—personal power.

Tier 1: Personal Power

This tier focuses on keeping your handheld communication tools powered during a short-term power outage. This is the easiest and most affordable starting point.

- **Scenario:** 1–2 days without power
- **Cost Range:** $200–plus

The goal of Tier 1 is to power personal communication tools for a short period of time. The low hanging fruit when it comes to power in this tier—at least for your tools that use them—is batteries. Many of the communication tools listed later, such as handheld radios, satellite phones, and emergency radios, all take batteries. While many tools are moving to rechargeable battery packs, batteries still have a place in your communications arsenal.

RECHARGEABLE VERSUS DISPOSABLE

When purchasing a backup supply of batteries to power your devices, opt for rechargeable versions versus disposable options where applicable. For popular batteries such as AAA, AA, and 9-volt, those labeled alkaline are single-use disposable batteries, whereas those labeled nickel–metal hydride (NiMH) and lithium-ion (Li-ion) are rechargeable. While NiMH and Li-ion both have slight advantages and disadvantages, both are excellent choices for powering handheld radios and/or emergency radios.

If a tool or device you choose uses traditional batteries such as AAA, AA, or 9-volt, a backup supply of rechargeable NiMH or Li-ion batteries is a wise investment. Be sure to have a compatible charger and matching power cord (USB preferred due to compatibility) to recharge the batteries using one of the power sources mentioned in the next sections of this chapter.

Battery Daddy storage case with AA and AAA USB battery charger.

BATTERY STORAGE

Although keeping batteries in their original packaging is a safe method of storage, it's not always the most convenient. A storage case designed specifically for this purpose can really help organize a large supply of batteries. While there are many on the market, a popular and affordable option is the suitcase-style Battery Daddy. This organizer accommodates seventy-eight AAs, sixty-four AAAs, eight 9-volts, ten Cs, twelve coin cells and eight Ds. It is also small, compact, and includes an integrated battery tester. Keeping your batteries organized and easily accessible will help to ensure you have turnkey power when the lights go out.

PROPRIETARY RECHARGEABLE BATTERY PACKS

Many devices now come with a proprietary rechargeable battery pack in lieu of over-the-counter replacement batteries. If you choose a communication device that includes one of these battery packs, consider purchasing a second battery pack as a backup. A fully charged backup battery can provide uninterrupted communication when the main battery runs out. It is also important to store all charging cords and charging docks for these unique batteries with your other communication tools so they are easy to find and access when needed. These tips will help ensure you have the means to recharge your devices during a power outage.

PORTABLE POWER BANKS

Portable power banks, such as the Anker 747 Power Bank, are small portable devices that can charge communication tools "on-the-go." They provide fast and easy power during an evacuation or when you're away from home. For example, this particular Anker 747 model in the photo can charge an iPhone five times, and most two-way radios multiple times, on a full charge reserve. These units are perfect for evacuation kits, bug out bags, or simply to have on hand for short-term emergencies.

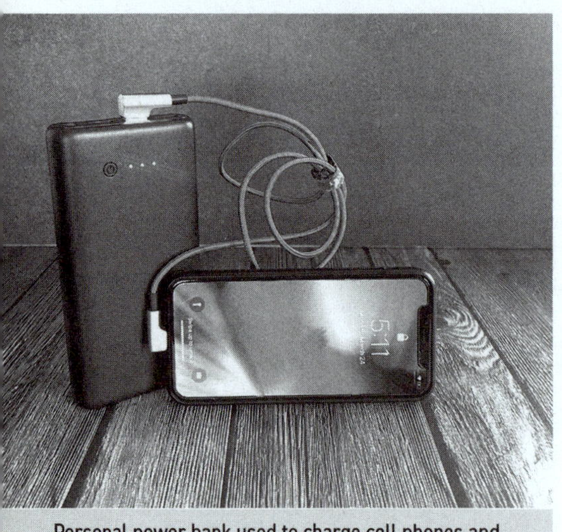

Personal power bank used to charge cell phones and other smaller devices.

PORTABLE "EVACUATION" SOLAR PANEL

In addition to a portable power bank, a lightweight folding solar panel that's designed for hiking and backpacking is a great addition to a bug out bag, evacuation kit, or short-term personal power kit. This can use renewable energy from the sun to power your communication tools or portable battery bank on the go. This ensures you can power or recharge your tools even while on the move.

A Goal Zero portable backpacking solar panel can be easily packed in a bug out bag to provide power while you're on the go. Find out more at https://goalzero.com.

PERSONAL POWER ACCESSORIES

Some power accessories are just as important as the power itself. Oftentimes, they are required to harness what power is available. Two critical accessories include:

- **USB charging cables:** You can never have too many of these. Many rechargeable radios and communication devices these days recharge via USB cable. Make sure to have several of the ones that are compatible with your devices for this purpose.
- **USB outlets:** If your generator does not have a USB charging outlet, be sure to have either a DC or an AC USB outlet that you can plug into your generator for charging your USB compatible devices.

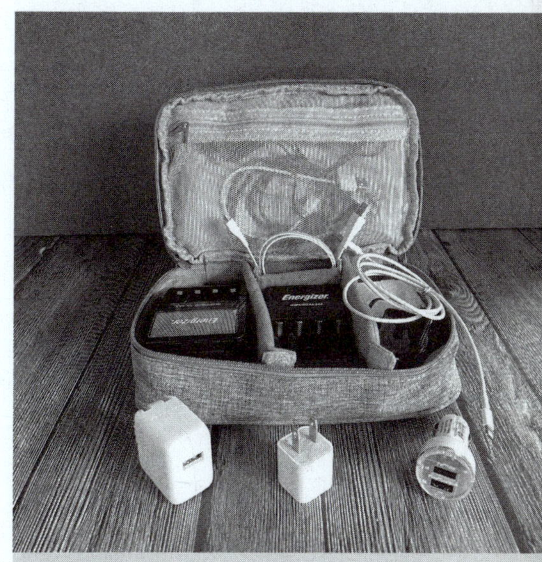

Communication power accessories including USB charging cables, AC USB outlets, and DC USB outlets.

Tier 2: Device Power Support

This tier is to help power larger tools, such as radios and laptops, for a multiday period while in a vehicle or at a mobile base camp.

- **Scenario:** Multiday power outage, vehicle communications, temporary base camp
- **Cost Range:** $1,000–plus

The goal of Tier 2 is to provide regular power to personal communication tools, such as cell phones, two-way radios, laptops, and more, for a multiday period. Tier 2 goes more into power generation than just storage, while remaining portable and cost effective.

18-VOLT MULTIUSE BACKUP BATTERY STATION

18-volt (18V) batteries are commonly used within the construction industry to power drills, saws, and other tools. These batteries are an incredibly flexible backup power option for communication devices and even household tools. Many brands, such as RYOBI, DEWALT, and Makita, have their own unique line of tools and accessories that are powered by 18V batteries. RYOBI, for example, has over three hundred different tools that can operate using their 18V battery. These tools include everything from vacuums and radios to drain snakes and circular saws.

Portable "power station" and drill that uses a RYOBI 18V One+ lithium battery as the power source.

While not designed necessarily for the communications industry, these 18V batteries provide a unique source of power to recharge communication tools such as handheld radios. Multiple batteries can also store a significant amount of backup power. Most brands have a "power station" that can allow a user to harness the power of the 18V battery using USB ports and a 110-volt outlet. The power station can then be used as a portable charging station for communication batteries and/or devices. In addition, the 18V batteries can be used with a variety of other useful household and construction tools.

However, because these power stations are also battery-based, they will eventually need a power source for charging as well. This brings us to some solutions for generating your own power when the traditional grid is down.

PORTABLE SOLAR GENERATOR

Portable solar generators are essentially smaller versions of the home power stations described later in this chapter. Ironically, amateur ham radio operators were at the forefront of this technology years ago before the newer plug-and-play options hit the market. Many operators built DIY versions of these units using ammo boxes, inverters, and batteries to provide power on the go for field operations. Luckily, the current off-the-shelf options are not only affordable and feature-rich but are perfectly suited to power a variety of the communication tools and devices discussed in later chapters.

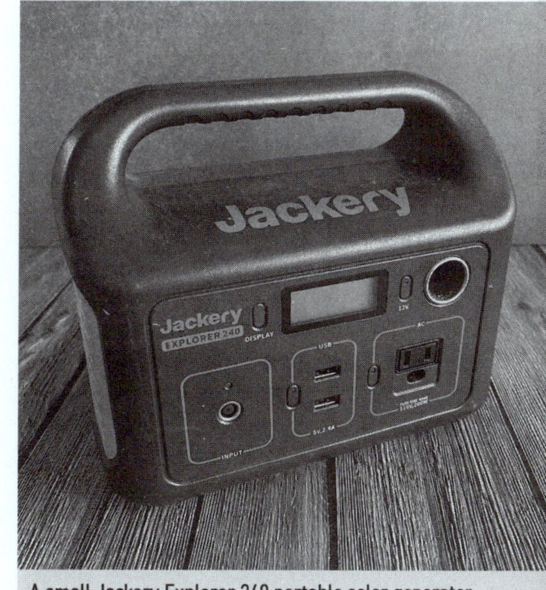

A small Jackery Explorer 240 portable solar generator.

A great example of a smaller portable solar generator is the Jackery Explorer 240 Portable Power Station, which can be purchased at the time of this writing for a little over $200. In this case, 240 denotes the generator's 240 watt-hour capacity. In layman's terms, watt-hours measure the amount of energy used or generated over time—like running a 1-watt device for 1 hour. This is an ideal power supply source for communication devices and tools at home or on the go. With a weight of 6.6 pounds, the Explorer 240 Portable Power Station can be easily carried around the house, stowed in a vehicle, packed in a bug out bag, or even carried by hand for communications in the field. It has a comfortable built-in handle for carrying. It is a very popular choice for off-grid power for campers as well.

The Jackery Explorer 240 Portable Power Station can be charged within 5 hours with a 100-watt solar panel. You can also power the portable solar solution with a wall outlet, generator, and car outlet. Jackery has numerous portable units like this that range in price and watt-hour capacity, depending on your needs.

PORTABLE GASOLINE- AND DIESEL-POWERED BACKUP GENERATORS

Portable gasoline- and diesel-powered generators are affordable and easy to operate. They are available for purchase at many different retailers, including home improvement stores and online. You can expect to pay $500 and up for a good gas-powered generator.

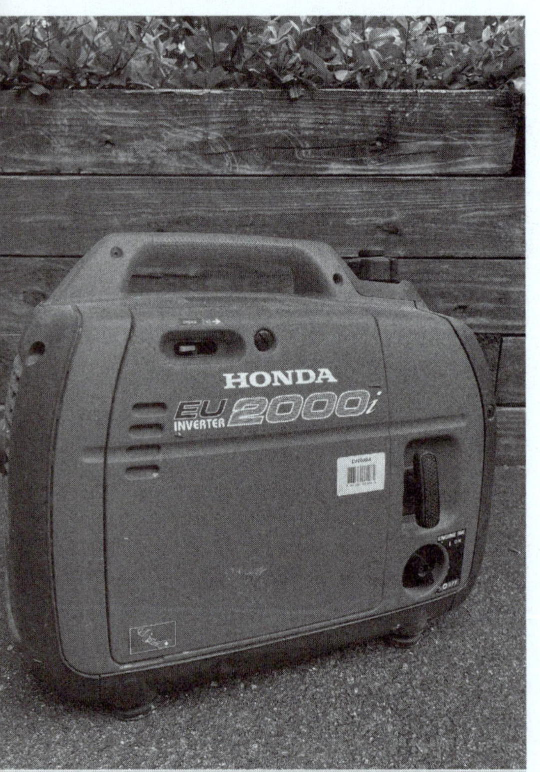

The small and quiet gasoline-powered Honda EU2000i Inverter Generator.

These types of generators are priced according to wattage. Every one of these generators will have the ability to power or recharge your communication tools. One important question to ask yourself when shopping for this type of generator is: Do you want to use it to only power your communication devices, or will you need it to power other items in your home, such as appliances? For Tier 2 power specifically, you'll focus on smaller generators that are more cost-effective and portable but offer less power.

One such generator is the Honda EU2000i, which outputs 2,000 watts of power. This generator is perfect for Tier 2 support and can easily run numerous smaller-load devices. Regardless of size, keep in mind that all gas-powered generators must operate outside because of carbon monoxide exhaust. You can power your home with this style of generator using two options: extension cords or a transfer switch. Transfer switches will be discussed later in Tier 3 support.

If you are using extension cords, you simply start your generator outside and run extension cords through an open door or window to the appliances or communication devices you need to power. However, this method has drawbacks. Not only is it messy, but using the wrong-sized extension cord can also be a fire hazard. If using this option, you should purchase what's called a generator cord, or gen-cord. This is an extension cord specifically designed to distribute the power from a generator. It plugs directly into the 20- or 30-amp plug on the generator (if available), and then you only have to run one cord into your home. The other end of the gen-cord splits into several standard 120-volt outlets where you can plug in items. With this option, you can only power items that you can plug into an outlet.

Gen-cord for safely plugging in multiple items using the 30-amp plug on a generator.

Gas-powered generators have one big drawback: You must have fuel to power them. Most portable generators will run 4–15 hours on one tank of gas, and this is highly variable depending on the model, size, and load. If you're considering this option, you will need to test your generator to see how long it will run on one tank of gas and then calculate how much gas you'll need to have on hand to power it for an ideal amount of time. When storing gasoline, use the fuel additive STA-BIL to extend the shelf life for long periods of time.

One nice aspect of this style of generator is that most of them are considered portable. Consequently, these are very popular among ham radio operators who set up communication hubs in the field during a crisis. As long as fuel is available, these generators are perfect for powering communication base stations and charging batteries. If space allows in your vehicle or on a hitch-rack or trailer, these generators can be taken with you in the event of an evacuation.

They can be used in temporary or semipermanent camps for powering radios and other items such as fans, phones, heaters, and flashlights.

Tier 3: Household Power Support

Larger 5,700-watt gasoline generator.

This tier focuses on multiday household-level power to keep your communication tools and household appliances online.

- **Scenario:** Extended grid-down event and loss of power
- **Cost Range:** $800–$5,000

Tier 3 power support is for those seeking to provide power to multiple systems for an extended period of time. This may include both communication tools and other household systems such as refrigeration or certain appliances. This category essentially includes larger versions of the items in the Tier 2 category that are capable of generating and/or storing more power for extended use. These include both fuel-powered and solar-powered generators.

LARGER BUT LESS PORTABLE: GASOLINE- AND DIESEL-POWERED BACKUP GENERATORS

While Tier 2 generators are chosen primarily for portability, Tier 3 generators are chosen primarily to support multiple home-level systems for an extended shelter-in-place scenario. The higher the wattage, the more powerful the generator and the more devices it will power. To give you an idea, an average home can be powered by a generator that can provide 5,000–8,000 watts of power. The price varies greatly depending on brand and power output.

For Tier 3 generator support, you will want to consider installing a transfer switch in your home. If you're not knowledgeable in this area, it is best to hire a local electrician to install this for you. This switch ties directly into your home electrical panel and allows you to send power not only to outlets in your home but also to appliances such as air conditioners, furnaces, ovens, and ceiling fans. A special type of gen-cord runs from your generator through a slightly open window or door and plugs into a receptacle on the transfer switch to send power. This is a more integrated approach to providing your home and communication tools with power. Reputable sources for power transfer switches are Generac, Reliance Controls, and EcoFlow.

Fuel Options and Storage

Choosing the right fuel for your generator can affect the shelf life and your readiness during a crisis. When preparing for longer power outages, you'll also need to prepare to have more fuel storage on hand if access to fuel from local sources is not available. It's important to understand what options are available and the differences in shelf life and storage guidelines. Typically, generators will operate on one of the four different kinds of fuel, although some generators can operate on multiple types of fuel. These fuels are gasoline, diesel, propane, and natural gas. Following are some things you should know about each of these different fuels.

Gasoline

- Shelf life (Untreated): 3–6 months.
- Shelf life (Treated): 1–2 years when a fuel additive (such as STA-BIL) is added.
- Storage container: Typically approved red 5-gallon plastic or metal containers.
- Ideal storage conditions: Cool, well-ventilated area away from any ignition sources.

Diesel

- Shelf life (Untreated): 6–12 months.
- Shelf life (Treated): 2 years with a fuel stabilizer and biocide additive.

- Storage container: Typically approved yellow diesel containers or metal drums.
- Ideal storage conditions: Cool, dry area away from sunlight.

Propane

- Shelf life (Untreated): Indefinite.
- Storage container: 20- to 100-pound tanks approved by the Department of Transportation or large stationary tanks from propane provider.
- Ideal storage conditions: Well-ventilated outdoor locations.

Natural Gas

- Shelf life (Untreated): Not stored—delivered through utility company via underground pipes.
- Special consideration: While natural gas is very dependable, it is susceptible to infrastructure damage as underground delivery pipes can be damaged during certain events, such as earthquakes.

SOLAR HOME BASE STATIONS

This category of backup power solutions is quickly becoming the most affordable and practical solution for many preparedness-minded individuals. This section can help you understand your options when it comes to large plug-and-play solar power solutions that do not require professional installation. Ten years ago, solar solutions were bulky, expensive, unreliable, and required professional skills to set up and operate. Now, thanks to advancements in solar and battery technology, there are a variety of very affordable plug-and-play options. There has also been a growing demand by people and various industries to have power and connectivity on the go and in remote locations, contributing to the shift toward solar solutions. Competition in the marketplace has driven prices (and sizes) down considerably in recent years.

Renewable energies (like solar and wind) are quickly becoming a favorite backup power category because, as the name implies, the energy is renewable. Unlike gasoline, diesel, propane, and natural gas, renewable energy isn't depleted once it's used. When it comes to solar power options, there is an assortment of choices, companies, brands, and power levels. Smaller, more portable solar generators have already been discussed in the Tier 2 category, but it's important to know there are only three main differences:

- **Size:** Home power stations are larger and weigh more, whereas portable units can easily be taken on the road and even stowed on a bicycle or in a backpack.
- **Power:** Home power stations offer more power storage and power output.
- **Price:** Home power stations are significantly more expensive than smaller, more portable units.

When it comes to Tier 3 power support, you'll be looking for the larger home base station models that offer both more power storage and more power output.

A solar home base station, while technically portable, is really designed to provide stationary power. Depending on the size, they can weigh 100-plus pounds. If space allows, they can be transported in a vehicle or used to power an RV or a remote camp. Their primary function is to power the electrical needs for an entire home, or at least the most important items such as refrigerator, lights, water pump, and furnace. They are entirely self-contained. They contain batteries that store energy for power and are oftentimes expandable to offer more power storage. You don't need to know anything about setting up solar charging systems because the technology, including inverters and outlets, are all built in.

Most solar home base stations have three options for charging: solar panels, plugging into a wall outlet in your home, or direct current from a vehicle. This gives you several options for keeping the unit charged before and during use. Many also have the option to plug into a transfer switch that connects to your home's electric panel and allows you to quickly and easily transfer power from the power station to your grid. This prevents you from having to plug a bunch of different things into the unit when the power goes out. You can decide which items from your home electric panel receive power from the transfer switch and then it's as simple as flipping a switch to provide power to them from your home base station.

An example of a home base station is the Jackery Explorer 3000 Pro Portable Power Station. With just over 3,000 watts of power, this 63-pound unit can power most homes. It's also portable, so it can be taken on the road to power an RV or off-grid camp. There is also an optional transfer switch. This particular unit charges by using solar panels, direct current (DC) from a vehicle, or by plugging it into a wall outlet. It takes 3–4 hours to charge by solar panels and about 2½ hours to charge by a wall outlet. At the time of this writing, the price of the base unit is $2,500–$3,000 but can exceed $7,000 with an added transfer switch and six 200-watt solar panels. This is the same price (or less) for what you can expect to pay for a propane or natural gas generator to power a whole house. But it uses renewable energy from the sun.

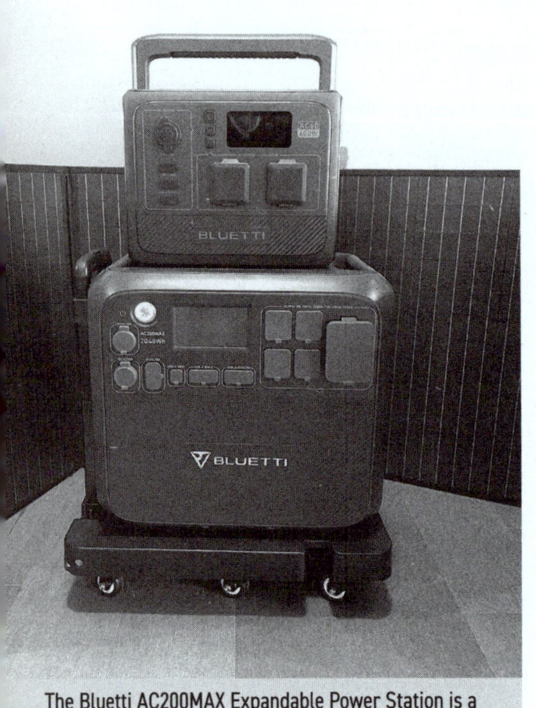

The Bluetti AC200MAX Expandable Power Station is a home base station that can be charged using solar, AC, and DC inputs.

One of the greatest benefits of a home base station is that it solves your communications power problem in addition to many other power problems as well, and it is a fantastic overall disaster-minded solution. But, of course, not everyone has a few extra thousand dollars to invest in a unit like this. Additionally, solar generators only make sense for you if you live in an area that gets consistent sun. If you live somewhere that's cloudy and rainy all the time, then keep in mind that this may not be the best option for you.

Tier 4: Whole-House Automatic Backup Power

Tier 4 focuses on automatic whole-house power for permanent and long-term resilience.

- **Scenario:** Long-term grid-down event and loss of power
- **Cost Range:** $5,000–plus

A Generac brand stationary whole-house propane-fueled generator.

Tier 4 power support is for those seeking a permanent, whole-home power solution. One of the most popular power choices in this tier is a stationary propane or natural gas–tied whole-house generator. This style of generator is hardwired to your home electrical panel and is designed to kick on as soon as power is interrupted. These generators require a natural gas feed or a large propane tank in order to operate. This style of generator is more than what is needed to power communication tools, but it is a great option for those seeking a solution that can handle all of their home power needs, communication included.

As you might imagine, hooking one of these up is a job for a professional, and you can expect to spend $6,000 or more for the generator and installation. These generators also require yearly maintenance to keep them running in tip-top shape, typically for an extra fee. And it's also wise to use them sporadically each month to ensure they are always in working order. Some electrical cooperatives have generator programs to help make buying one a little easier. Call your local electric company and see if they have any incentives or provide installation.

The main advantage of these generators is that they provide backup power for your entire home. Natural gas is one of the most reliable fuels during a disaster, and if you have a propane tank, you can run this type of generator for a long time, especially if used intermittently. The disadvantages are that you're still dependent on fuel, and the unit and installation are pricey. This type of generator is also fairly big, so it's not an option for apartment dwellers and others who live in tight quarters in a city. This type of generator is also not portable.

Rotating and Maintaining Your Backup Power Supply

Just like any tool or stored supply item (like a bug out bag or long-term water storage), your power tools and fuel storage are equally dependent upon routine maintenance and rotation. This section will help to make sure your equipment doesn't fail when you need it most. Here are some recommended maintenance items with timelines to keep your power category in tip-top shape.

- **Keep batteries charged:** Whether it's your cell phone battery bank, your 18-volt battery storage, or your solar generator, it's important to keep the batteries charged. If they sit unused, the charge will slowly diminish and it is a good idea to charge them back up at least once per month. For lithium batteries, do not leave them charging continuously, but rather just top them off once per month. For NiMH or lead-acid batteries, occasional charging or using a trickle charging tool is recommended to keep them in optimal working order. A trickle charger, or battery maintainer, provides a constant gentle charge which keeps the battery charged and in good health.
- **Generator use:** Be sure to use all generators at least once every couple of months. This ensures they are ready for action in the event of a power outage. Make sure to use the batteries in solar generators and start the engines of fuel-powered generators. Recharge and fill up fuel after usage.
- **Fuel rotation:** Set a reminder on your phone to rotate fuel storage every 6 months for gasoline (1 year if treated) and every 12 months for diesel (2 years if treated). This ensures your fuel will be effective when needed.

You now have several options, depending on your goals, to keep your communication tools powered. From harnessing the sun's energy with solar panels and battery storage to utilizing gasoline-powered generators, these tools ensure you have electricity (power) during a crisis. They can make all the difference when the grid goes down.

Quick Action Checklist

Use the following checklist to identify the items you want to add to your Tier 1–4 power plans.

Tier 1

- ❑ Battery types
  - AA
  - AAA
  - 9-volt
  - Unique rechargeable battery packs specific to devices
  - Other: ______________
- ❑ Battery charger
  - Compatible battery charger
  - Power cords
- ❑ Storage container
  - Battery Daddy or similar storage unit
- ❑ Proprietary rechargeable battery packs
- ❑ Personal portable power bank
- ❑ Portable "evacuation" solar panel
- ❑ Extra USB charging cables
- ❑ Extra USB charging plug (AC)
- ❑ Extra USB charging plug (DC)

Tier 2

- ❑ 18-volt batteries/charger/power station
- ❑ Portable solar generator plus solar panels
- ❑ Portable gasoline- and diesel-powered backup generator
- ❑ Fuel storage
- ❑ Gen-cord

Tier 3

- ❑ Larger gas or dual-fuel generator
    - Transfer switch
    - Gen-cord
    - Fuel storage
- ❑ Larger solar home base station with high watt-hour capacity
    - Transfer switch
    - Solar panels

Tier 4

- ❑ Stationary whole-home propane or natural gas–tied generator

PART 2

RADIO COMMUNICATION

Part 2 of this book focuses on the critical role radio communication plays in staying connected during disasters. While the usual communication tools such as cell phones, Internet, and social media are great, they are often the first to disappear during widespread disasters. This often leaves individuals and communities without reliable means of contact. Radio operates outside of cellular infrastructure and Internet services and has proven to be effective during countless disasters. Even when modern communication infrastructure fails, radio still works.

In the following chapters, you'll learn about different radio services, various radio setups and the communication options they offer, as well as how to maximize their effectiveness. In addition, this part will highlight when and where certain radios make the most sense. We'll also cover more advanced topics like boosting signal range, selecting appropriate frequencies, and operating radios efficiently. By the end of this part, you'll be able to confidently choose the communication tools that make the most sense for you and your family, ensuring you can stay connected, informed, and in control when it matters most.

Whether you're a beginner who's never touched a radio, a radio owner who's just getting started, or an experienced ham radio enthusiast, the tips, advice, and information in this section will help you integrate radios into your family or group emergency communication plan and gain clarity for which radios best fit your goals.

CHAPTER 4

BASIC RADIO TECHNOLOGY AND SERVICES

In this chapter, you'll learn the foundational elements of radio technology and how to choose the radio services that make the most sense for your own goals and circumstances. Whether you're creating a communication plan for your family or hope to deploy in a disaster, the knowledge gained in this chapter will be beneficial to both.

Radio Technology

Understanding how radios transmit and receive information is foundational to not only using them but also troubleshooting them in a disaster. Two-way radios operate by transmitting and receiving radio waves. These radio waves are called carrier waves because they carry information, such as voice, data, or music. Attaching information to a carrier wave is called modulation. Two-way radios use either amplitude modulation (AM) or frequency modulation (FM). In addition, there are two subsets of AM transmissions: upper sideband (USB) and lower sideband (LSB). Each modulation has its advantages and disadvantages.

Radio waves carry information via modes. Modes include analog voice, digital voice, digital data, and constant wave.

- **Analog voice** radio communication is the most common and well-known mode.
- **Digital voice** works by converting analog voice information into digital information transmitted as a data stream; it is then decoded back into audio information by the other radio.
- **Digital data** radio communication is generated by a computer connected to a radio. The radio transmits data in radio waves, which are then decoded by a radio and computer at the other end.
- **Constant wave** radio communication is used for Morse code.

Radio Frequencies

Different radio frequencies have pros and cons, so understanding each one can help you decide which frequency makes the most sense for your location and desired communication goals. Radio waves are composed of oscillating electric and magnetic fields. The electric and magnetic fields are perpendicular to each other. So, if the electric field is vertical, the magnetic field is horizontal, and vice versa. The electric field indicates a radio wave's polarity and follows the long axis of a radio antenna. At the basic level, a vertical antenna emits a vertically polarized radio wave, and a horizontal antenna emits a horizontal radio wave.

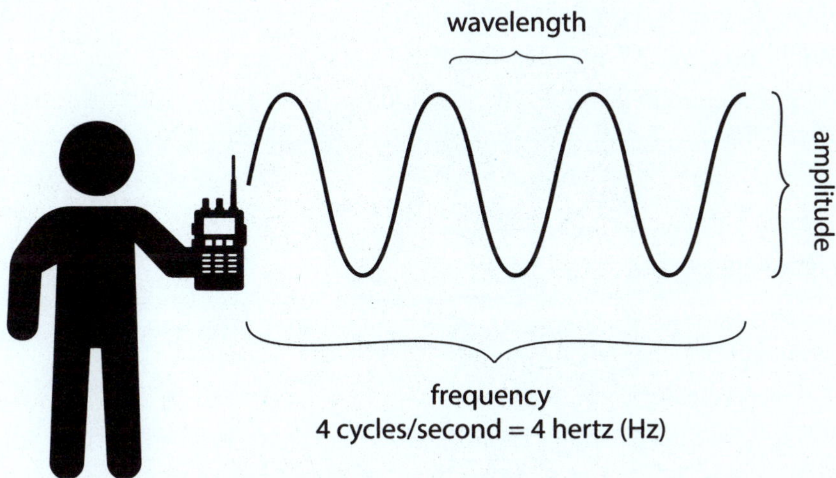

Vertical polarity radio waves emitting from a vertical antenna.

Two-way radio operators use three primary frequency ranges: high frequencies (HF), very high frequencies (VHF), and ultra high frequencies (UHF). Each radio service (discussed in the following sections) is limited to operating in one frequency range, except ham radio, which has operating privileges in all three ranges.

Each frequency range has unique properties. Some frequencies provide very long transmission distances but are susceptible to interference. Others work well in urban and obstruction-dense environments but are limited in transmission range.

HIGH FREQUENCIES (HF)

High frequencies (HF) provide the longest radio communication distance (about hundreds to thousands of miles between radios). Skywave, sometimes called skip propagation, makes this long-distance communication possible. The ionosphere—the upper atmosphere that sits hundreds of miles above the Earth's surface—refracts or bends radio waves at specific frequencies back toward Earth. This is similar to how light bends when it passes through water. HF radio waves refract and travel a particular distance depending on the sun's interaction with the ionosphere. The time of day, time of year, and where the sun is in its eleven-year solar cycle all affect HF propagation.

During normal times, HF communication is the most reliable radio means to contact family and friends living hundreds to thousands of miles away. This is possible because HF radio waves (skywave propagation) skip over obstructions and geographic features (such as buildings and mountains) and past the horizon. Ham radio is the only civilian two-way radio service with substantial access to the HF radio spectrum.

High Frequency Pros:

- Farthest reach (from local to global communication)
- Abundance of frequencies
- Greater versatility
- Will survive a solar flare or coronal mass ejection (CME) which can cause an electromagnetic pulse (EMP) all of which can affect the Earth's magnetic field.

High Frequency Cons:

- Unpredictable signal quality
- Comparatively large radios and antenna systems
- Greater power consumption
- Expensive
- High learning curve

VERY HIGH FREQUENCIES (VHF)

Very high frequencies (VHF) radio waves propagate along a line of sight and are limited by the horizon, trees, buildings, mountains, and other obstructions. The harder it is for the transmitting and receiving antennas to see each other, the harder it is for them to hear each other. Putting the antenna on a tower, roof, or mountain can help overcome these limitations. The higher the antenna, the farther the signal can travel.

VHF radios are excellent for outdoor use. VHF radios can reach down the street, across town, or under the right conditions from state to state. Simple modifications and upgrades to your antenna can extend the range of even low-powered VHF radios.

The majority of emergency radio communication occurs on VHF. Firefighters, EMTs, and police, as well as boat and airplane pilots, use VHF radios for communication. VHF line-of-sight propagation is more reliable and predictable than HF communication, which is why it is relied on for these life-and-death situations. Also, all ham radio operators are permitted to use an extensive range of VHF frequencies, so more people use it. That increases the chance of someone being on frequency to answer a call for help.

Unlike HF radio waves, VHF radio waves are rarely refracted by the ionosphere but punch right through it into outer space. VHF's ability to propagate through the ionosphere is why NASA uses VHF radios to communicate with the International Space Station.

Very High Frequency Pros:

- Smaller radios and antennas
- Resilience to interference
- Low power needed
- Easy to use
- Access to monitor first responder, aircraft, maritime, and FM broadcast frequencies

Very High Frequency Cons:

- Limited reliable transmitting range
- Vulnerable to obstructions
- Limited frequencies

ULTRA HIGH FREQUENCIES (UHF)

Ultra high frequencies (UHF) radio waves are similar to VHF, but don't travel as far as VHF. However, UHF waves are short enough to pass through walls, making them an excellent choice for operating inside buildings and other structures.

Ultra High Frequency Pros:

- Smallest radios and antennas
- Resilience to interference
- Low power
- Easy to use
- Less susceptible to obstructions; works well in structures

Ultra High Frequency Cons:

- Most limited transmitting range
- Limited frequencies
- Shorter battery life

SELF-ASSESSMENT

Based on the previous information, think about which frequency range best matches your daily and emergency communication goals.

- Do you primarily want to stay in touch with neighbors, or do you have friends and family long distances away?
- Do you live in a downtown urban area, an open rural space, or a mountainous terrain?
- How would your environment affect line of sight?

An Overview of Personal Radio Services

Choosing the right radio service starts with the basics of understanding the rules, options, limitations, and how each of these applies to public and personal use. Each country has its own communication regulatory agency. The Federal Communications Commission (FCC) regulates radio communication in the US, including broadcast radio (FM and AM stations), first responder radio, personal radio, and many others. The FCC separates personal radio use into services and determines the parameters for using the radio services, including maximum transmitting power (watts), modulations and modes, general radio construction, appropriate operating practices, and license requirements. In this section, you'll learn about the various personal radio services to decide which ones are best for your Family Communication Plan.

You might already be familiar with some of the personal radio services, such as Citizens Band (CB), Family Radio Service (FRS), and amateur (ham) radio. The FCC established these services for two-way radio communication between everyday citizens. As the name implies, two-way radio permits people with radios to talk back and forth over short or long distances without connecting wires. Other people may be listening in, but the intention is for two people to communicate directly at a time. Two-way radio communication is like fishing with a pole. You stand on the shore and cast your lure into the water to attract and catch a fish. Other fish might see the lure, but usually, only one takes the hook. Once it does, it's just between you and the fish.

Another standard classification of radio is broadcast radio. You probably listen to broadcast radio in your car. Broadcast radio is like fishing with a net. You cast your net into the water and catch as many fish as possible; in other words, you cast a broad net. A broadcast radio signal comes from one station to your radio and hundreds or even thousands of others, but no one can talk back directly to the radio station. The talk show host will never hear you, no matter how loudly you yell at the radio in your dashboard.

Most of the discussion in this chapter will be about two-way radio. However, broadcast radio provides essential information during local, regional, and large-scale disasters, so the next chapter will circle back to that topic.

A license is not necessary to monitor or listen to any radio service, even ham radio and General Mobile Radio Service (GMRS), but it is required to transmit on those services. In fact, monitoring first responder, aviation, marine, and business frequencies is allowed by law because airwaves are considered public, but how you use that information is regulated and varies at the local, state, and federal levels. Also, many first responder radios use digital voice technology, which isn't available to the general public. In this case, if you tune to a first responder frequency, all you'll hear is hissing or something similar to the squawking and squealing of an old dial-up modem.

You can monitor many first responder, aviation, ham, and utility frequencies without a radio. You may be able to monitor digital transmissions as well. There are websites and apps that stream radios tuned to local frequencies. Several of these include:

- **RadioReference.com** and its spin-off site Broadcastify provide information about radios around the world. RadioReference.com provides a searchable database of frequencies used by first responders, municipalities, airports, government agencies, and others. Broadcastify is a streaming service that allows users to monitor radios around the world, many of which are listed in the RadioReference.com database. Both have forums for users to exchange information about interesting radio transmissions.
- **GlobalTuners.com** is one of the original remotely controlled radio sites on the Internet. It primarily streams HF and shortwave receivers, but some VHF and UHF receivers are also available. The interface mimics the controls of a physical receiver, so using it can be good practice before you shell out cash for a receiver. Chat boxes also allow you to interact with other users listening to the same radio.
- **KiwiSDR.com** is similar to GlobalTuners.com but uses software-defined radios (SDR). There are hundreds of KiwiSDR receivers distributed

around the world. SDRs aren't as intuitive as traditional radios but can simultaneously accommodate several listeners monitoring separate frequencies.
- **5-0 Radio Pro Police Scanner and Police Scanner Radio & Fire** are Apple iOS and Android apps. They stream audio from police, public safety, aeronautical, and ham radio frequencies. Many of their streams originate from Broadcastify or RadioReference.com. Both apps offer free and paid options.

Personal Radio Services: The Breakdown

This section will help you choose which specific radio service best matches your communication needs and goals. There are five personal radio services regulated by the FCC:

- Amateur (ham) radio
- General Mobile Radio Service (GMRS)
- Family Radio Service (FRS)
- Citizens Band (CB)
- Multi-Use Radio Service (MURS)

Ham radio, GMRS, FRS, and CB are the most applicable for family emergency disaster situations. MURS is too limited in power and frequency options to be beneficial for most family emergency use.

AMATEUR RADIO SERVICE (HAM RADIO)

Amateur radio, often called ham radio, can communicate worldwide with even modest gear. It also has access to all three primary frequency ranges: HF, VHF, and UHF. Ham radio signals are capable of neighborhood, regional, and worldwide communication, making them suitable for any scenario. However, passing an exam to earn a license is necessary for operating a ham radio, so it may not work for you. The good news is that non-licensed persons may speak on ham radios as long as a license holder is present at the controls.

Ham radio also provides the most modulations: analog voice, digital voice, and digital data. You can send emails, texts, and social media posts to non-ham friends and family. Pictures and faxes can also be transmitted and received with a ham radio.

Ham radio use requires a license that is earned by passing an exam. There are three classes of licenses for new hams, each with its own exam: Technician, General, and Amateur Extra. The entry-level ham radio license is the Technician Class, which has the lowest frequency access. These are primarily in the VHF and UHF ranges and some HF. General Class licensees have the same VHF and UHF privileges as Technicians, plus a wide range of HF access. Amateur Extra Class licensees have full access to all ham radio frequencies.

Established hams who help people get started in ham radio are called "Elmers." Almost every city, town, or county has a ham radio club where you can find an Elmer. The best clubs are usually associated with the American Radio Relay League (ARRL). Look up a club at www.arrl.org and visit them. Hams are always eager to welcome you into "the hobby."

Ham Radio Pros:

- Robust
- Flexible
- Local and global communication
- Highest powered (up to 1,500 watts)
- Widest variety of modulations and modes
- Can monitor all other services (broadcast, aviation, marine, first responder, etc.)
- Can transmit, with radio modification, on all other services

Ham Radio Cons:

- Higher cost
- Learning curve
- License requirement
- Complex gear and setup
- Commercial use prohibited

Before buying a ham radio, consider these points:

- Do you have the interest and discipline to study for and take the ham radio license exam?
- Do you want the ability to send emails, texts, and even images as a part of your Family Communication Plan?
- Would you benefit from accessing all three frequency ranges (HF, VHF, UHF) in a single radio service?
- Are you looking for the most versatile and powerful system, even if it costs more and requires more study?

Why Earn a Ham Radio License?

People often ask, "Why can't I buy a ham radio but not use it until after the end of the world as we know it? Nobody will care that I don't have a license after society and the government collapse." Imagine purchasing a firearm to provide food and protection but never practicing with it before it's needed. Many well-intentioned people have followed this philosophy, but unfortunately, they'll learn that even though ham radios aren't tricky to use, they require practice. They will have spent hundreds, even thousands, of dollars on radio gear that will be expensive paperweights if they didn't practice with it before it's needed.

So, where to start? If you're interested in pursuing a ham radio license, try Joe's Ham Cram course on OutdoorCore.com. It includes six hours of on-demand video training, along with video conference coaching sessions and direct access to an experienced personal trainer, available through email. There's a six-hour course for the Technician Class (entry-level) license and one for the General Class (mid-level) license. Hundreds of people, some as young as ten years old, have earned their licenses with this course, so give it a try at www.outdoorcore.com.

GENERAL MOBILE RADIO SERVICE (GMRS)

Imagine this scenario: A group of five families is prepared with GMRS radios and a repeater on a hill separating them. Each family has a GMRS license, base radio, mobile radio, and a walkie-talkie for each family member. A squall line of severe thunderstorms and tornadoes wipes out local communication infrastructure, but each family and their family members maintain contact until local utilities restore services.

GMRS makes for a pretty good disaster communication plan. GMRS requires a license but doesn't require passing an exam and while the licenses are issued to individuals, they apply to all immediate family members. GMRS is channelized for ease of use and uses FM modulation for excellent audio. There are thirty GMRS channels, all in the UHF range; twenty-two are used for direct radio-to-radio communication, and eight are reserved for repeater use. GMRS and FRS radios conveniently share frequencies and can communicate with each other. Voice transmissions on GMRS are analog only, but short digital data transmissions (texts and GPS information) are permitted with walkie-talkies. A downside is that GMRS transmission distances are limited mainly by line of sight. UHF radio waves can pass through walls and vegetation, but they are still attenuated or inhibited by obstructions such as mountains and large buildings.

In terms of equipment, there are walkie-talkies, mobile, and base GMRS radios. Most GMRS walkie-talkies have 5-watt output power—mobile and base radios are limited to 50 watts. Directional, or gain, antennas can increase transmitting ranges significantly. Repeaters can significantly increase the range of GMRS radios. GMRS repeaters can be found in most moderately dense population centers. They're also found in areas popular with hunters, off-road enthusiasts, and other outdoor adventurers.

When considering using GMRS, think about these points:

- Is your goal to communicate easily with your family or neighbors within a 1–10-mile radius?
- Is "no test required" more important than range and power to you?
- Are you comfortable with paying for a one-time license to cover your whole family?
- Does the use of GMRS repeaters to increase your communication distance sound like something you are interested in?

GMRS Pros:

- Ease of use
- More power = increased range
- No exam necessary
- Excellent audio quality

- Repeaters permitted
- Allows digital data transmissions on walkie-talkies (but not base or mobile radios)
- Commercial use permitted

GMRS Cons:

- Limited frequencies available (channels)
- Limited range compared to radios with equal power
- License required
- License expense
- Regulations can be confusing

FAMILY RADIO SERVICE (FRS)

The Family Radio Service (FRS) is a licensed-by-rule service, meaning you can use it if you follow the rules. It shares frequencies with GMRS, which is handy for interoperability. FRS radios are limited to either 2 watts or 0.5 watts, depending on the frequency. Neither the radio nor the antenna can be modified. If you've ever bought walkie-talkies at a big-box store, they were probably FRS radios.

When thinking of purchasing an FRS radio, consider these points:

- Do you need simple, license-free handheld radios for kids, elderly family members, or less-trained users?
- Are your communication goals mostly short range (household, cul-de-sac, campground)?
- Do you see value in supplementing your more powerful radios with inexpensive backups for untrained team members?
- Would FRS radios help during an evacuation scenario where short range is sufficient and simplicity matters most?

FRS Pros:

- Ease of use
- Inexpensive price point
- No exam or license required
- Readily available

FRS Cons:

- Limited range
- Less durable
- Walkie-talkie only

CITIZENS BAND RADIO SERVICE (CB)

Citizens Band (CB) radio is popular with truckers and long-distance motorists. It's a licensed-by-rule service, which means you can use it if you follow the rules. CBs are also popular with hikers, off-roaders, and families using them to stay in touch.

CB radios transmit in AM or single sideband (SSB), which can be either upper sideband (USB) or lower sideband (LSB); however, not all CB radios have SSB capability. There are forty CB channels near the top of the HF range. Channels are predefined frequencies. For example, Channel 19 is predefined for the frequency of 27.185 megahertz (MHz). It's easier to remember and tune "19" than "27.185." These channelized frequencies make CB radios easy to use, but at the expense of limited options.

The CB transmission power limit is 4 watts for AM and 12 watts for SSB, which limits CB radio's range to 15 miles in an unobstructed line of sight. However, 2 miles is a more realistic distance for reliable communication. CB antennas can be interchanged, modified, and upgraded to increase transmitting range.

If you are thinking about buying a CB radio, consider these points:

- Do you often travel on rural roads or highways where CB radio use is common?
- Are you looking for a short-range backup communication option that doesn't require a license or Internet?
- Would you benefit from a radio service that allows you to contact mainly road-bound individuals if you ever get into a bad situation (like truckers or roadside assistance)?
- Is ease of use, accessibility, and affordability more important to you than advanced features?

CB Radio Pros:

- Affordable
- Low learning curve
- Business use permitted
- Synonyms (handles) and "10 codes" (see Chapter 6) permitted
- Inexpensive
- Commercial use permitted

CB Radio Cons:

- Limited range
- Voice only
- Radio modification prohibited
- Significant interference from other stations
- No privacy (or PL) tones (see Chapter 7)

Quick Action Checklist

Use the quick action checklist that follows to take some steps toward choosing the best radio option for your needs.

- ❑ Examine the environment around your home base and identify primary obstructions like hills, mountains, buildings, and trees. Consider how these might affect line-of-sight radio communication, and which frequency (HF, VHF, or UHF) might be best for your circumstances.
- ❑ Clearly define your communication goals by deciding whether you are most interested in communicating locally, regionally, or nationally for both daily use and emergency applications.
- ❑ Based on the information from the previous two points and the pros and cons listed in this chapter, decide which frequency best serves your needs: HF, VHF, or UHF.
- ❑ Narrow down the list of radio services (ham, GMRS, FRS, CB, MURS) to one or two options that best fit your goals and needs. Make a point to consider cost, range, and license requirements.

- ❑ If ham radio is included in your list from the previous point, log onto www.arrl.org to find a local ham club. Consider attending a meeting for training and support.
- ❑ Based on your radio service choices, begin to create a starter gear list of items you'll need to gather or buy. Include things like antennas and accessories for portability and power needs.
- ❑ If you've chosen ham radio or GMRS, think about when might be the right time to pursue licensing.

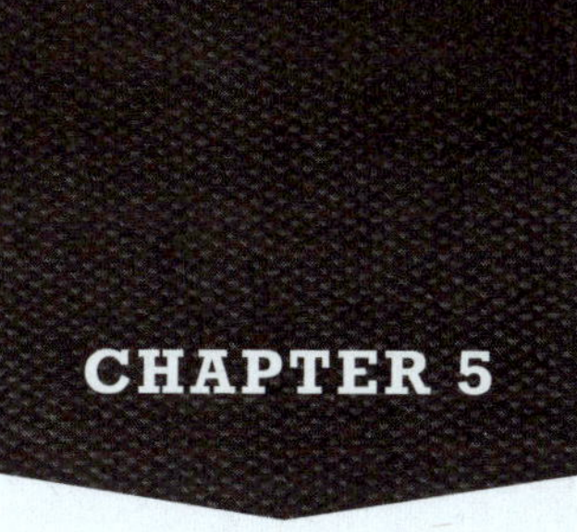

TYPES OF RADIOS

History proves that radio technology is the most resilient, robust, and reliable form of electronic communication. It's the only electronic communication tool that does not rely on any infrastructure. Even satellite Internet, phones, and texting devices rely on an infrastructure of satellites and "earth stations" that can be rendered inert by solar storms, human error, and cyberattacks. But radio is the only true off-grid solution. Learning the different types of radio setups can help you narrow down which ones best meet your needs, budget, and communication goals. This chapter will explain the basic radio setups and help you choose the right radio gear to include in your Family Communication Plan.

Two-Way Radio Components

Two-way radios have two main components: a transmitter and a receiver. Years ago, the transmitter and receiver were separate components, but now they are combined into a transceiver unit. The transmitter encodes sound from an input device, such as a microphone, Morse code key, or computer, into radio waves and transmits them from an antenna. As the name implies, the receiver receives incoming radio waves through an antenna and decodes them back to sound you can hear through a speaker or data you can read on a computer screen. Car radios, weather radios, police scanners, and TVs are all examples of radio wave receivers. (The terms "radio" and "transceiver" will be used interchangeably for this section.)

Transceivers come in four basic configurations:

- Handhelds (walkie-talkies) that you can carry.
- Mobile radios mounted in an automobile.
- Base stations installed at home.
- Portable or go-kits.

The upcoming sections will recommend radios that reflect each service's features, specifications, and price. Use this information and the quick action checklist at the end of the chapter to research and select the best gear for your emergency communication strategy.

Note: When looking at a radio's output power, it's good to know that twice the output power doesn't equal twice the transmitting distance because of the inverse square law. If 5 watts cover a 2-mile radius, 10 watts will cover a little less than 3.

Handheld Radios

Handheld radios are the most basic radio stations. In order to select the best one for your family or team, it is worth taking the time to learn what options exist and understand the associated strengths and limitations of each. These radios are also known as walkie-talkies, handy-talkies, or HTs. We'll refer to them as handhelds throughout this chapter.

An emergency radio operator's handheld transceiver is their most personal piece of radio gear. If you're having difficulty choosing between two models with similar features, select the one that you find easy to operate, appeals to your eye, or simply "feels right." Please don't dismiss this point. You won't use a piece of gear you don't like, and the less you use it, the less confident you'll feel using it under distress in an emergency or a disaster.

FAMILY RADIO SERVICE (FRS)

The Retevis RT45P Waterproof Walkie-Talkie is a robust, no-frills radio that offers everything you need and none of the extras you don't. Unlike other FRS radios, the RT45P has a respectable IP67 rating, making it one of the most durable radios on the market. (IP ratings indicate an electrical device's water and dust protection.)

Inexpensive FRS handheld radios are perfect for "cul-de-sac" communications.

GENERAL MOBILE RADIO SERVICE (GMRS)

When it comes to GMRS radios, both the Retevis Ailunce HA1G or Radioddity GM-30 Plus are excellent options. The HA1G is robust, with a relatively high dust and water-repellency rating (IP67). The GM-30 has an internal GPS and can share coordinates with other GM-30 Plus radios.

GMRS radios have detachable antennas that can be swapped out for gain antennas that extend the transmitting and receiving range.

Joe's tried and true Yaesu FT-60R.

The Cobra HH RT 50 Road Trip can be used as a handheld or mobile radio.

AMATEUR RADIO (HAM RADIO)

The Yaesu FT-60R is the radio Joe carries in his everyday carry, bug out bag, and go-kit. He's taken it on numerous hurricane deployments, and it still works like brand-new.

CITIZENS BAND (CB)

Handheld CB radios can be connected to an external antenna to improve transmission range. The model pictured in the photo on the right (Cobra HH RT 50 Road Trip) comes standard with a magnetic mount antenna that can be mounted on the roof of a car or truck.

Mobile Stations (Vehicle Installations)

The term "mobile" means mounted on or in a motorized vehicle. These setups typically offer more power and range. Most mobile transceivers are powered by a 12-volt DC power source, usually the automobile's battery. This section will help you understand the various setups so you can decide which is best for your needs. Whichever radio you select will need to be properly installed in your vehicle. Many two-way radio dealers and car stereo installers provide professional installation services. Local ham radio club members will be happy to recommend trusted professional installers in your area.

FAMILY RADIO SERVICE (FRS)

FRS radios are handheld only with permanently attached antennas, so they are ineffective for mobile installations.

GENERAL MOBILE RADIO SERVICE (GMRS)

The BTECH GMRS-50V2 has up to 50 watts of output power, which is the full legal limit for GMRS. It receives National Oceanic and Atmospheric Administration (NOAA) and FM broadcast radio and scans, and can act as a repeater. It scans UHF and VHF frequencies but transmits only on assigned UHF frequencies. We recommend matching it with a Midland MicroMobile MXTA13 replacement antenna.

CITIZENS BAND (CB)

The President McKinley is a solid radio for everyday CB communication and performs well in single sideband (SSB) mode. FCC allows 12 watts of output power in SSB mode for CB use. That's three times more than is permitted in AM mode. Also, SSB signals travel farther than AM signals at the same power output. That extra range is essential in an emergency.

Mobile CB radios usually come with mounting hardware and power cables. This one is ready to be installed.

Additionally, the Wilson 305-38 (Little Wil) mobile CB antenna is an excellent value.

AMATEUR (HAM) RADIO

Following are the two most popular ham radio mobile installations: Dual-band VHF/UHF and multiband HF/VHF/UHF. (As the names imply, dual-band radios can operate on two distinct frequency bands and multiband radios on three or more.

This mobile ham radio station provides short, medium, and long-distance communication while traveling. The picture shows the control heads only. The actual radios are located under the seats to save space. The top unit controls a 100-watt HF transceiver, and the lower unit controls a dual-band VHF/UHF radio.

Dual-Band VHF/UHF

The Icom IC-2730A is a 50-watt dual-band transceiver with an easy-to-read display and large controls that are laid out well. It comes with scanning capability, NOAA radio/alert, and Bluetooth.

A good mobile antenna is the Comet MA-721, a magnetic mount dual-band antenna with a PL-259 connector for attaching to your mobile radio and an SMA adapter for use with a handheld radio.

HF/VHF/UHF

We recommend buying a used HF/VHF/UHF radio. The Icom IC-706MKIIG and Yaesu FT-100D are favorites with emergency communicators. They can be purchased "pre-owned" to save money. Both come with removable faceplates that let you mount the radio under a seat, in the trunk, or some other out-of-the-way location. Neither radio has an internal tuner. We recommend the LDG AT-100ProII.

For antennas, we recommend the Comet MA-721 for VHF/UHF and the Opek HVT-400B for HF.

Base (Home) Stations

Home base stations can be an anchor-hub for disaster communication or everyday monitoring. Mobile transceivers, like the ones previously mentioned, are a great way to start your home base station. Just add a 12-volt DC power supply, mount an antenna outside your house, connect the radio to the antenna, and you'll be on the air in no time.

It's important to note that any necessary electrical upgrades to your home should be done by a licensed electrician in accordance with local codes. Also remember that your antenna height is limited according to the radio service used, geographic location, local laws, and construction codes.

GENERAL MOBILE RADIO SERVICE (GMRS)

The BTECH GMRS-50V2 with a BTECH RPS-30M power supply is the same radio we recommended for mobile setups. Its 50-watt output power is the full legal limit for GMRS radios, and it comes with all the features you need to get started in GMRS emergency communication. In addition, the Comet CA-GMRS is an excellent gain antenna that's tuned specifically for GMRS frequencies.

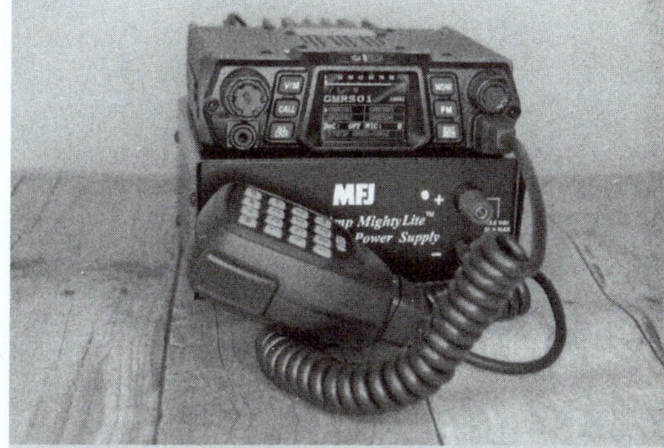

This GMRS mobile transceiver also works as a base station when attached to a 12-volt power supply.

CITIZENS BAND (CB)

To set up a CB base station, you will use a 12-volt power supply to power the radio and a base antenna tuned for CB frequencies. The President McKinley makes an excellent CB base station when powered by a Pyramid PS14KX 12-amp power supply. The ProComm Proton PT99 antenna is inexpensive and easy to install.

AMATEUR (HAM) RADIO

An HF/VHF/UHF all-mode transceiver is best for a home station, and buying used is a good way to save money. Connect your radio to a dual-band VHF/UHF antenna and an HF wire dipole antenna to complete the station. The IC-706MKIIG, Yaesu FT-100D, or Kenwood TS-2000 all work well as base station transceivers. The TS-2000 allows you to monitor two frequency bands at the same time, while the IC-706MKIIG and FT-100D do not. If you prefer to buy a new radio, the all-band, all-mode Yaesu FT-991A is an excellent radio. Unfortunately, it doesn't provide simultaneous dual-band operation.

The Samlex SEC-1223 power supply pairs well with any of the previously mentioned setups. The Diamond X200A Dual-Band VHF/UHF and Moonraker G5RV HF antenna would both work well in this setup.

Joe's home ham radio setup (pictured in the photo) may likely be more complicated than the average person's or the beginner wishing to set up a disaster communications position. However, seeing this example allows you to imagine what is possible when it comes to a ham radio setup at home.

Joe's main ham radio operating position.

Joe's setup includes: The radio in the middle is a 100-watt HF transceiver used mainly for voice and digital transmissions. To its left is a 40+-year-old radio that uses both transistors and tubes. On the right side of the desk is a 12-volt, 30-amp power supply that powers the HF/VHF/UHF radio sitting on top of it. On top of that radio is a manual antenna tuner, and on top of the tuner are two audio interfaces for digital communication. Joe uses this equipment to send and receive email via radio waves using the Winlink Global Radio Email system (Winlink is detailed in Chapter 8). All three monitors are connected to the same PC. All radios in the "shack" can be controlled with the software displayed on the right-hand monitor. Directly beneath the right computer monitor is a VHF/UHF transceiver used to scan police, fire, and utility frequencies. The center monitor displays Doppler radar and a visual representation of radio transmissions received at an Internet-connected remote receiver. The left monitor displays hurricane tracking and prediction software the author uses to make decisions regarding radio operator deployment.

HOME BASE RADIO INSTALLATIONS

Each two-way radio installation is unique with far too many variations to list and describe in this book. However, most do-it-yourselfers are capable of installing a basic station. Of course, upgraded and more complicated installations (increased power, antenna towers, routing wires through walls, etc.) may require professional skills. The authors encourage you to contact a local ham radio club for advice before installing a base radio station.

Portable Stations (Go-Kits)

Go-kits are portable radio stations used for emergency and disaster communication. If your goals are to have a disaster-ready portable communication hub to deploy at any moment, this section will help ensure you have everything you need in one package for both power and communication. Go-kits typically have more transmitting power than a handheld radio and can be carried to places, such as disaster zones, where a vehicle cannot go. Any of the mobile radios previously listed can be used in a go-kit.

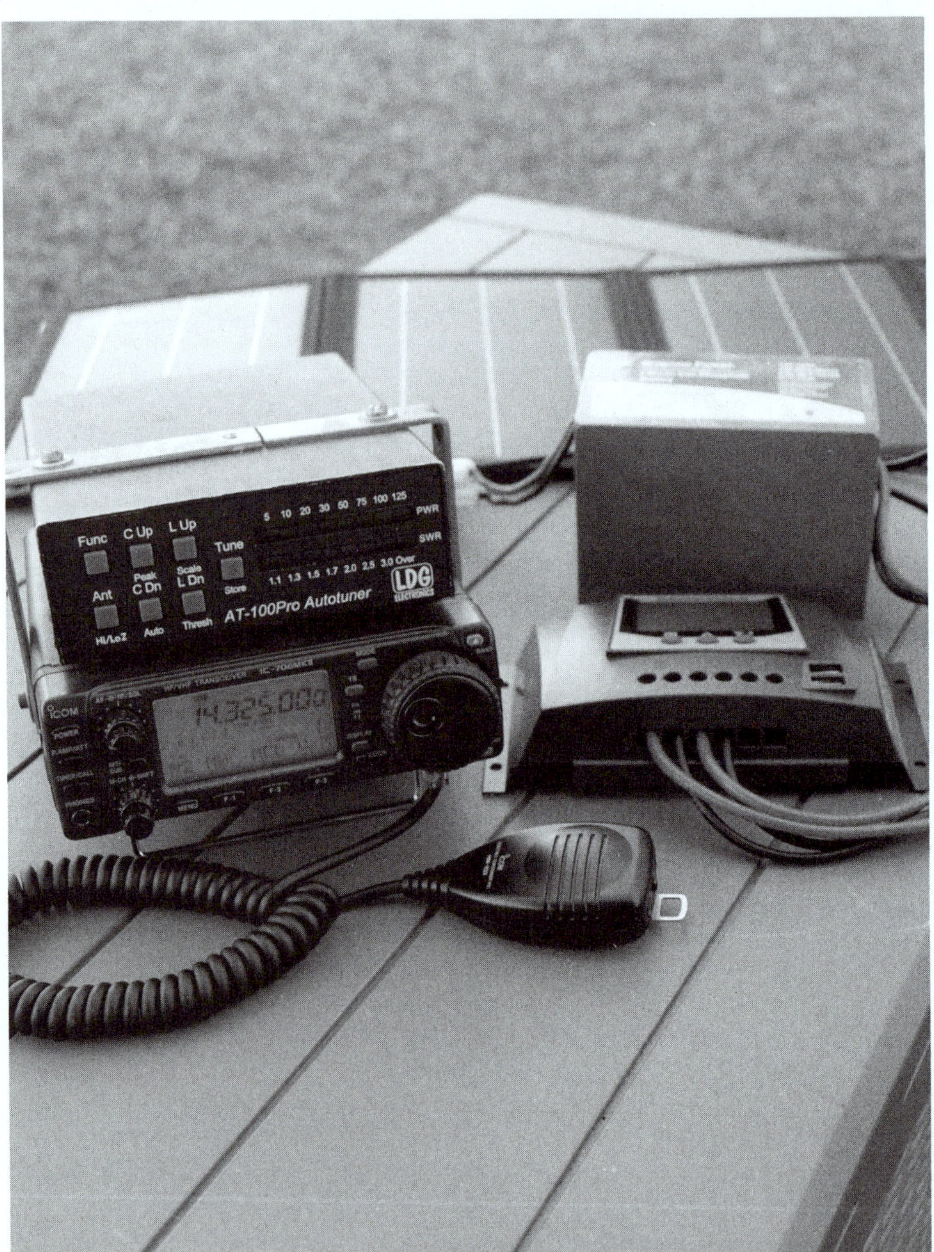

A 12-volt, 15-amp-hour lithium-iron phosphate battery and 28-volt solar panel provide up to 8 hours of operation for this HF/VHF/UHF ham radio go-kit. Notice the external antenna tuner mounted on top of the radio.

A good go-kit is scalable and can be adapted to meet the situation. It might start with a handheld and mag mount antenna that fits in a backpack. When you're ready to upgrade, just add a mobile VHF/UHF radio, an appropriate power source, and an upgraded antenna. You now have a go-kit capable of communication in the most likely bug out, evacuation, and disaster situations. And it's an excellent bug in station too.

Here's a list of generic components in a sample go-kit:

- HF/VHF/UHF 100-watt mobile ham transceiver
- 12-volt, 23-amp AC-DC power supply
- VHF/UHF 5-watt walkie-talkie with NOAA radio and police/fire scanning capability
- GMRS walkie-talkie
- Handheld CB radio
- Wire HF antenna
- VHF/UHF vertical base station antenna
- Two 75-foot lengths of 50-ohm coax
- A molded plastic, dust/waterproof, briefcase-style case

Have an assortment of connectors in your go-kit: various terminal connectors, including SO-239 barrel connectors, PL-259 to SO-239 elbow connectors, SMA to SO-239 and BNC to SO-239 adapters, 1-foot coax connectors, and so on.

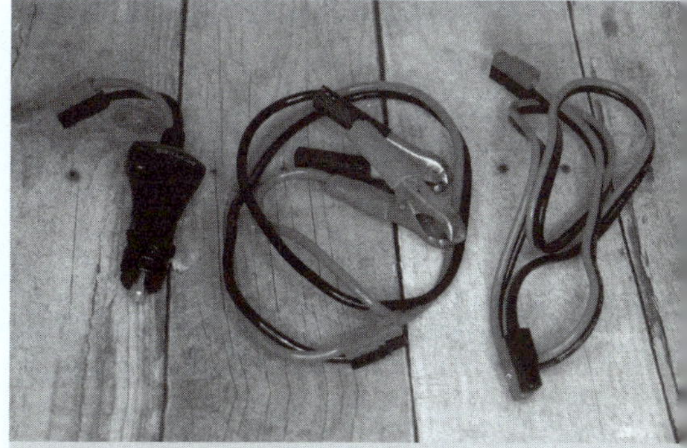

Install Powerpole connectors on power cords. Powerpole interconnectivity is helpful when sharing or swapping radio gear. These are some cable alternatives using Powerpole connectors.

Several companies sell pre-built go-kits. Shack-in-a-Box (https://shack-in-a-box.com) provides preconfigured turnkey and custom-built products. If you'd like to build your own go-kit, check out Scott Roberts's book titled *How to Set Up Your "Perfect" Amateur Radio Go-Kit*. It's written for ham radio go-kits, but the principles and concepts apply to other personal radio services.

Joe's HF/VHF/UHF Shack-in-a-Box rack-mounted go-kit.

A Family Emergency Disaster Radio Setup

This section will help you choose a radio setup that's perfect for your family or team. With levels for minimal, basic, or ultimate, you'll learn how to create a setup that matches your goals, skill level, and budget. GMRS and ham radio VHF/UHF radios are best for family emergency communication within a 10-mile radius. GMRS's family licensing, shallow learning curve, and low cost make it the perfect entry point and backbone for family emergency radio communication. But if you go the extra mile and add a ham radio station, your family can stay in touch and be informed to and from anywhere in the world. We recommend that FRS, MURS, or CB radios play a secondary role in your emergency communication plan.

Following are three checklists that will help you get started in purchasing equipment to set up a reliable family emergency communication setup. These are broken down into minimal, basic, and ultimate configurations to fit your needs and goals.

Minimal Family Emergency Disaster Radio Setup

- ❑ GMRS handhelds: one per adult
- ❑ FRS radios: one per child
- ❑ Antennas: one GMRS mag mount for use with adults' handhelds

Basic Family Emergency Disaster Radio Setup

- ❑ GMRS handhelds: one per family member
- ❑ GMRS mobile: one as previously described
- ❑ GMRS base: one as previously described
- ❑ Option: additional GMRS mag mount antenna to be used as a backup with a handheld
- ❑ Enhanced: GMRS repeater (setup is outside this book's scope)

Ultimate Family Emergency Disaster Radio Setup

- ❑ GMRS handhelds: one per family member
- ❑ GMRS mobile: one per vehicle
- ❑ GMRS base: one as previously described
- ❑ GMRS repeater
- ❑ Ham: at least one licensed family member who is at least sixteen years old
- ❑ Ham handhelds: one dual-band VHF/UHF per licensed member
- ❑ Ham mobile: one VHF/UHF as previously described per licensed member
- ❑ Ham base: one HF/VHF/UHF as previously described

When thinking about your family emergency disaster radio setup, consider these points:

- How many people do you realistically want to have a radio in your household or team?
- Do you have a radio budget in mind?
- Which setup best aligns with your communication goals: minimal, basic, or ultimate?
- Do you have an area in the house to set up a communication base station?
- Do you have a vehicle that could be used as a mobile comms station?
- Can you mount a base station antenna at your home or in a discreet way?

Hybrid Radio Technology

This section will discuss radio devices that rely on both wired and wireless technology. We refer to it as "hybrid radio technology" because it doesn't fit neatly into the definition of radio, but it's important that you at least know what it is.

DIGITAL VOICE (DMR, C4FM, D-STAR)

Digital voice is an exciting and fun technology in the ham radio community. Digital voice transmissions are largely interference-free with a strong signal, pictures can be sent between radios with internal cameras, and radios can be connected to the Internet for global communication. Despite the possibilities, digital voice technology has yet to prove itself widely deployable in disaster scenarios.

ECHOLINK (VOIP)

EchoLink is a radio frequency–Voice over Internet Protocol hybrid technology available to licensed ham radio operators. The free EchoLink program is available for Windows, iOS, and Android platforms. It connects hundreds of ham radios around the world through the Internet. Ham radio operators use the EchoLink program or app to connect to remote transceivers tuned to specific frequencies in the ham radio bands, usually VHF. Using their computer microphone, they can talk to other ham radio operators virtually anywhere. They can also use their radios to connect to EchoLink nodes through local repeaters connected to the EchoLink network.

CELLULAR-BASED RADIO (LONG TERM EVOLUTION, OR LTE)

Cellular-based radios operate like walkie-talkies but use all available cellular networks—such as Verizon, AT&T, and T-Mobile. When one network is unavailable, these radios

Cellular-based radios can communicate worldwide but rely on infrastructure.

automatically switch to another, which gives communication options beyond a single provider. Cellular-based radios are not limited to distances or lines of sight. The most significant drawback is that they rely on infrastructure. Another is that other people in your party must also have one to communicate with.

Receivers

Thus far, this chapter has discussed numerous options for radios that can send and receive messages. However, there is an entire category of radios that are used for gathering information only. These are called receivers, and they play a unique role in emergency communications where every bit of information gathered can help to make more educated and thorough decisions.

These devices can help you build situational awareness in a disaster and make better, more informed decisions. When you are thinking about buying a receiver, consider what kinds of updates are important to your communication goals during and after a disaster, for example:

- Local weather alerts (NOAA)
- General situational awareness about important events (AM/FM or shortwave)
- Real-time updates from local first responders such as police and fire

TRANSISTOR RADIO

The humble battery-powered transistor AM radio is the most basic receiver during a disaster emergency. Every well-prepared family should have one. These radios can receive emergency broadcasts, local news updates, weather alerts from the National Weather Service (NWS), and even evacuation notices—even when cell service and the Internet are down.

NOAA WEATHER RADIO ALL HAZARDS

Every well-prepared family also has a NOAA Weather Radio All Hazards. Features to look for include AM/FM, weather alert and radio bands, multiple power sources (battery, solar, hand crank), USB charger for smartphone, alarm clock, and flashlight. The Eton American Red Cross FRX3+ has all of these features in a rugged case at a reasonable price point.

The Eton American Red Cross FRX3+ Emergency NOAA Weather Radio can be powered by a rechargeable battery, hand crank, or solar panels in the handle.

SHORTWAVE RADIOS

A well-equipped shortwave radio receives AM and FM broadcasts, shortwave broadcasts, and HF ham SSB radio transmissions in a lightweight package with a small footprint. Additional features include channel memory, variable tuning step size, an alarm clock, and a backlit screen. An external antenna improves reception. The Tecsun PL-330 is an excellent shortwave radio with all of those features. It's portable and packable with a USB rechargeable battery.

Joe uses this Tecsun portable shortwave radio mainly for nighttime entertainment when backpacking, but it has also proved invaluable on disaster communication deployments.

In addition, the Raddy RF919 Shortwave Radio is a nice, albeit pricey, receiver with NOAA weather band reception and SSB capabilities. It also receives VHF, UHF, Air, and CB frequencies. It has a microSD card slot and Bluetooth and can be controlled with a smartphone app.

SCANNERS

Scanners sequentially scan preselected channels or frequency ranges. They stop and activate the speaker when a signal is detected. They then resume scanning after a predetermined period or once the signal is no longer present. These signals can be analog or digital, conventional or trunked modes. Analog scanners won't work when scanning digital systems, but many can scan multiple modes.

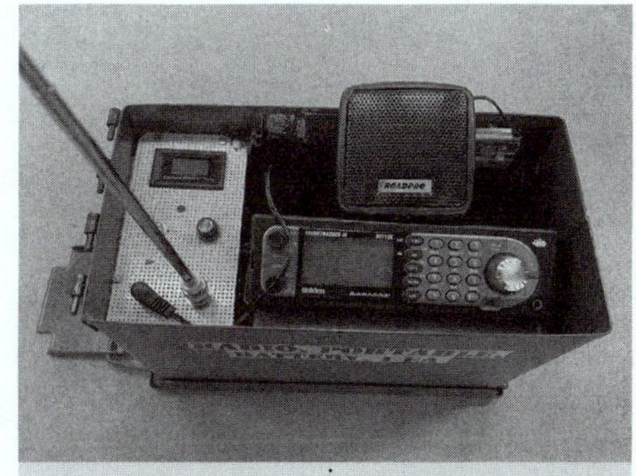

This radio (police) scanner, battery, and external speaker are mounted in an ammo can go-kit. Ammo can go-kits work with small-footprint GMRS and VHF/UHF ham radios.

Choosing a scanner depends on what the police department, fire department, utilities, and so on use in your area. Some scanners automatically find and save relevant frequencies. Others are programmed manually or by computer. RadioReference.com, mentioned in Chapter 4, is an excellent source for finding interesting frequencies in your area.

An external antenna will increase any radio's reception. This handheld scanner is attached to an antenna mounted outside Joe's house. It's connected to the 50-ohm cable with a BNC to SO-239 adapter.

A scanner's most critical feature is search/scan speed, and in terms of this, the faster the better. Other features include alpha tagging (assigning short descriptions to channels) and computer programming. Some models are directly compatible with RadioReference.com and will automatically populate channels from the RadioReference database.

The Uniden BC365CRS is an excellent analog scanner for the price. For a digital scanner, consider the Uniden Bearcat BCD260DN.

Quick Action Checklist

It's time to decide which radio setup(s) you want to add to your communication toolbox. Use the information in this chapter and the quick action checklist that follows to determine what radio setups make the most sense for your circumstances.

Personal Radio Services (Two-Way Communication)

		Expense	Range (miles)	Frequencies
Handhelds	FRS	$50-$75/pair	2	Moderate
	GMRS	$75-$100/pair	5	Moderate
	CB	$75-$125	5	Moderate
	Ham	$75-$200	5-10	Extensive
Mobile	GMRS	$150-$250	20	Moderate
	CB	$175-$250	2-10	Moderate
	Ham VHF/UHF	$300-$400	15-30	Large
	Ham HF/VHF/UHF	$500+	Global	Extensive
Base	GMRS	$200-$400	35	Moderate
	CB	$200-$400	20	Moderate
	Ham VHF/UHF	$400-$500	35	Large
	Ham HF/VHF/UHF	$500+	Global	Extensive
Go-kit	GMRS	$150-$250	35	Moderate
	CB	$175-$250	2-10	Moderate
	Ham VHF/UHF	$300-$400	35	Large
	Ham HF/VHF/UHF	$500+	Global	Extensive

Receivers

- ❑ Transistor radio (for receiving Emergency Alert System (EAS) public warnings)
- ❑ NOAA Weather Radio All Hazards (for receiving NOAA weather radio broadcasts)

Installation	Learning Curve	License	Exam
None	Easy	None	No
None	Easy	$35 per family	No
None	Easy	None	No
None	Moderate	$35 per person	Yes
Moderate	Easy	$35 per family	No
Moderate	Easy	None	No
Moderate	Moderate	$35 per person	Yes
Difficult	Elevated	$35 per person	Yes
Moderate	Easy	$35 per family	No
Moderate	Easy	None	No
Moderate	Moderate	$35 per person	Yes
Extensive	Elevated	$35 per person	Yes
Moderate	Moderate	$35 per family	No
Moderate	Easy	None	No
Moderate	Moderate	$35 per person	Yes
Moderate–Difficult	Elevated	$35 per person	Yes

- ❏ Police scanner (to monitor local police, fire and rescue, marine, aeronautical, and utility messages)
- ❏ Shortwave radio (for receiving global radio updates and messages)

CHAPTER 6

BASIC RADIO OPERATION

In this chapter, you'll learn the core skills every disaster communicator needs to know, regardless of radio service or radio type. Any piece of gear is only as good as the operator. From basic operation and choosing a frequency to extending range and using repeaters, an accomplished radio operator understands their radio's capabilities, controls, and how to get the most out of them. This chapter will teach you the technical aspect of two-way radios, including basic radio settings, frequency/channel selection, power levels, and antenna use.

Basic Radio Controls

Before communication can take place, you must understand what all the buttons on your radio do. All radios have the same basic controls: an on/off button or switch, volume knob, squelch/RF gain knob, tuning knob, push-button keypad, display screen, and a push-to-talk (PTT) button. They also have input and output devices, usually a microphone and a speaker.

- **On/Off button or switch:** Used to turn the radio on and off; it's sometimes part of the volume knob.
- **Volume knob:** Adjusts the loudness of the speaker.
- **Squelch/RF gain knob:** Squelch mutes unwanted weak signals and static below a certain threshold, and the RF gain finely adjusts radio signals. Squelch is used primarily with FRS, GMRS, MURS, and CB (AM)

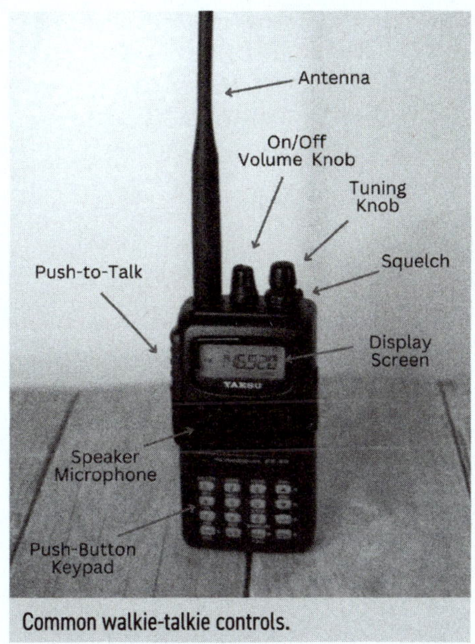

Common walkie-talkie controls.

transmissions. It also applies to AM and FM ham radio signals. RF gain applies to CB and ham radio SSB transmissions. Since AM and FM are the most common modulations used for line-of-sight propagation, this chapter will deal primarily with squelch control.

- **Tuning knob:** Used to select a channel or frequency. In ham radio, you might hear it called a VFO (variable frequency oscillator).
- **Push-button keypad:** Used to directly input channel, frequency, PL tone, menu selections, and so on.
- **Display screen:** Displays radio settings such as channel/frequency, PL tone, power level, battery life, and so on.
- **Push-to-talk (PTT) button:** When depressed, this button disengages the speaker, engages the microphone, and puts the radio in transmit mode. When released, it re-engages the speaker and puts the radio in receive mode.

The layout of these controls differs from model to model, but they are usually laid out intuitively. For instance, the tuning knob is usually the largest control, and the squelch control is often a ring around the volume knob. Radio manufacturers generally follow these conventions for walkie-talkies, mobile, and base stations. Refer to your radio's manual for specific control locations.

Here are some points to consider on radio controls:

- Have you located and read the manual for each of your radios?
- Can you identify and use all the basic controls on your radio (on/off, volume, squelch, tuning, PTT)?

- Do you know what each control does and how to adjust it for clear transmission and reception?
- Do you know how to set the volume, squelch, and frequency for your radio?
- Do you know how to use the accessories with your radio such as headphones, microphone, or external speaker?
- Can you successfully program your radio in the field without using programming software?

Selecting a Frequency

Choosing the right frequency is critical to getting your message to go through. Some frequencies travel better in a straight line, and others refract or bend. Some follow the earth's curvature, and others interact with the upper regions of the atmosphere, particularly the ionosphere. Some resist atmospheric interference, while others are less robust. Some easily penetrate solid walls but are limited in transmitting distance, and others can travel thousands of miles with less power than a 50-watt light bulb. (In this section, the words "channels" and "frequencies" will be used interchangeably. Just keep in mind that "channels" are like nicknames for "frequencies.")

Radio wave propagation describes how a radio wave travels. Line-of-sight and skywave are the two most common forms of propagation for emergency and disaster communication. Line-of-sight propagation occurs when radio waves travel in a straight line between antennas that can "see" each other. It covers the shortest distance. The majority of disaster and emergency communication travels by line-of-sight propagation.

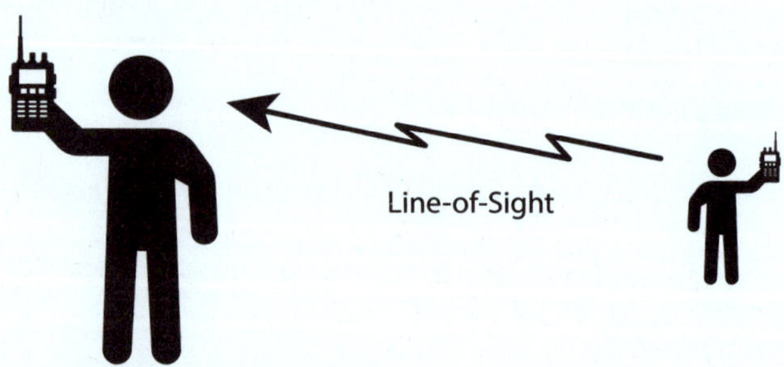

Skywave propagation (skywave for short) occurs when radio waves travel up to the ionosphere from an antenna mounted at ground level and are refracted back to a distant earthbound antenna. Skywave propagation makes interstate, international, and intercontinental radio communication possible. There are two primary forms of skywave propagation: low-angle skywaves and Near Vertical Incidence Skywaves (NVIS).

Skywave propagation occurs when radio waves are refracted by the ionosphere hundreds of miles above the Earth's surface then return to a receiving antenna hundreds or even thousands of miles away. A "skip zone" that doesn't receive the radio signal is created between the transmitting and receiving radios.

CHOOSING A LINE-OF-SIGHT FREQUENCY (VHF/UHF)

Most communication happens over line-of-sight frequencies. Learning how to use them for clear communication, even when obstacles are present, is critical. No line-of-sight frequency is more effective than any other, assuming that both allow the same maximum power output. However, more power equals more transmitting distance, so two 50-watt GMRS mobile stations cover more area than two 5-watt GMRS handhelds on the same frequency. Also, two-way communication is limited to the coverage of the weakest radio signal. A 5-watt radio will hear a 50-watt radio 15 miles away, but the 50-watt radio won't hear the 5-watt radio.

A good rule is to select a frequency that allows the maximum power output for that radio service. No one has exclusive use of any frequency in the personal radio services. They're "first come, first served," so listen before transmitting, then ask, "Is anyone using this frequency?" Scripted out, the process would look like this:

1. Assemble the radio according to the manufacturer's instructions.
2. Turn on the radio.
3. Turn the squelch knob fully counterclockwise. (This will allow you to hear static.)
4. Set the volume knob to a comfortable listening level.
5. Turn the squelch knob clockwise until the static or background noise is no longer heard.
6. Set the radio for the maximum power allowed on that channel.
7. Use the tuning knob or keypad to enter the desired frequency or channel.
8. Use the keypad to enter the appropriate PL tone, if necessary (see later in this chapter).
9. Listen for 10–20 seconds. If no one is heard, proceed to step 10. If you hear someone using the frequency, select another channel and try again.
10. Hold the radio's microphone about four fingers away from your mouth, push the PTT, pause for a second, then ask, "Is anyone using this frequency [include your ham or GMRS call sign, if necessary]?" Release the PTT and listen for several seconds.
11. Repeat step 10.
12. If no one answers after your second request, you're ready to start communicating.

CHOOSING A SKYWAVE FREQUENCY

Skywave frequencies can help reach someone hundreds or thousands of miles away. Skywave applies to ham radio in the high frequency range. (Skywave occasionally occurs on CB frequencies or VHF, but it's unreliable for emergency and disaster communication.)

Low-angle skywave usually transmits one thousand to several thousand miles over the horizon. In doing so, it creates a skip zone that is thirty to one thousand miles in radius from the transmitter. The signal isn't heard in the skip zone. This is why a station two hundred miles away might not be heard, but a station twelve hundred miles away is. Unfortunately, the help you need in a disaster is usually within one to five hundred miles of the affected area, too far for line of sight and too close for low-angle skywave.

Near Vertical Incidence Skywave (NVIS) is the most effective skywave propagation for disaster communication because it reaches the skip zone. As the name implies, NVIS signals launch almost straight up from the antenna and then are refracted back toward Earth by the ionosphere.

Low-angle skywave is like a garden hose with a high-pressure sprayer. If you hold the sprayer parallel to the ground, the stream of water lands several feet away. NVIS is holding the sprayer vertically; the water stream goes up and then returns to the ground much closer to you.

Skywave communication can be complex and depends upon many variables, so we won't do a deep dive into it here. However, skywave propagation is necessary for radio communication with family and friends more than one hundred miles away and might fit into your Family Communication Plan.

UNDERSTANDING FREQUENCIES

When contemplating frequencies, consider these questions:

- Do you understand the difference between channels and frequencies?
- Can you explain line-of-sight and skywave propagation in simple terms?
- Are you choosing frequencies that match the range you need in a disaster situation?
- Have you practiced the full step-by-step process for selecting and testing a frequency?
- Do you know what skip zones are, why they matter in emergencies, and how to overcome them?

A dipole antenna setup for NVIS communication. Notice the two "legs" (wires) extending to the right and left. Suspended at full height (40 meters high), its signal would transmit thousands of miles. Erected at about 3 meters high, as in this picture, the signal transmits almost straight up and down, covering the area within 500 or so miles.

Extending Your Radio's Range

There are instances when you'll need to communicate farther than your radio can do on its own. There are three primary methods to extend your radio's range. The most obvious is to use more power, which is limited according to the radio service used. The next is through the use of repeaters. The third is using a directional antenna, sometimes called a gain.

HOW TO USE A REPEATER

Repeaters are automated radios that retransmit a signal. GMRS and ham radio are the only services that allow repeaters. The most common repeaters are duplex, meaning they use two frequencies: one to receive the signal and one to retransmit (repeat) it. Simplex repeaters, which use one frequency for receiving and transmitting, are rare and aren't addressed in this book.

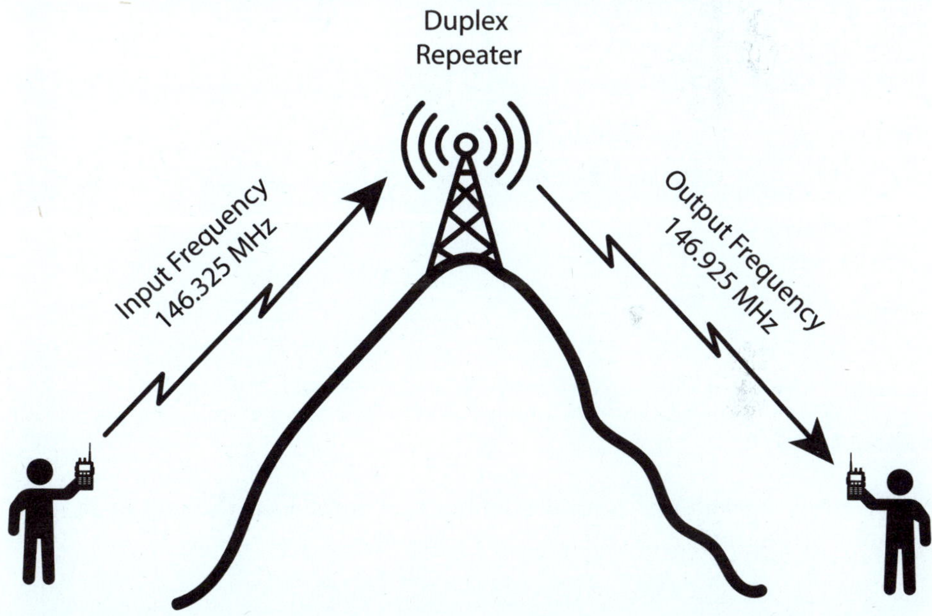

Extending communication range over a mountain with a duplex repeater.

Repeaters can use the full output power allowed with antennas 100 feet or more aboveground, significantly increasing the range of a transceiver by tens or hundreds of miles. They're set up and owned by radio clubs, civic organizations, and individuals, but are usually open for use by any radio operator in that particular radio service. The process for using, or "connecting" to, a repeater is similar for both GMRS and ham radio. Both require simple radio programming according to the manual for your particular radio.

Connecting to a GMRS Repeater

Connecting to a GMRS repeater will allow you to communicate much farther. First, find a repeater near you at https://mygmrs.com/repeaters and note the repeater's frequency and PL tone, if any. Match the three digits to the right of the decimal in the repeater frequency with the digits to the right of the decimal in the frequencies in the "Frequency" column that follows. Then, note the matching channel in the left-hand column. This is the channel that you'll tune your radio to.

Channel	Frequency
RPT15	462.550
RPT16	462.575
RPT17	462.600
RPT18	462.625
RPT19	462.650
RPT20	462.675
RPT21	462.700
RPT22	462.725

Note: GMRS repeater frequencies are aligned with the standard or simplex GMRS channels 15–22. Also, each radio manufacturer indicates repeater channels differently. Refer to your radio's user manual for channel designations.

The steps that follow demonstrate how to set up a GMRS repeater-capable radio to use a repeater on a frequency of 462.650 and PL tone 141.3.

1. Refer to the previous chart to find the channel that corresponds with frequency ###.650.
2. Frequency ###.650 is repeater Channel 19 (or Channel 27, depending on the manufacturer).
3. Turn on the radio.
4. Turn the squelch knob fully counterclockwise. (This will allow you to hear static.)
5. Set the volume knob to a comfortable listening level.
6. Turn the squelch knob clockwise until the static or background noise is no longer heard.

7. Set the radio for the maximum power allowed on that channel.
8. Using the channel dial or keypad, tune the radio to the repeater channel you found in step 2 (RPT19).
9. Using the process described in your radio's manual, set the PL tone to 141.3. Some manufacturers number the PL tones sequentially, i.e., tone 67 is #1, tone 69.3 is #2, etc. A chart will be included in the radio's manual.
10. Press the PTT and say your call sign into the radio's microphone, then release the PTT.
11. If your settings are correct, and the repeater is in range of your radio, you should hear a beep, tone, or short static burst. You might also receive an answer from another GMRS radio operator!

Connecting to a Ham Radio Repeater

Ham radio repeaters can give you incredible reach. You need the repeater's input *and* output frequency to connect to a ham radio repeater. The difference between those two frequencies is called an "offset." The good news is that most high-quality ham radios have the offset preprogrammed, so all you need to enter is the repeater's output frequency. You will also need to know the repeater's PL tone, if any. Ham radio repeater information can be found at www.repeaterbook.com.

The steps that follow demonstrate how to set up a ham radio to use a repeater with an output frequency of 146.925 MHz, a –.600 offset, and a PL tone of 156.7.

1. Turn on the radio.
2. Turn the squelch knob fully counterclockwise. (This will allow you to hear static.)
3. Set the volume knob to a comfortable listening level.
4. Turn the squelch knob clockwise until the static or background noise is no longer heard.
5. Set the radio for the maximum power allowed on that channel.
6. Use the dial or keypad to tune your radio to the repeater's output frequency, 146.925 MHz.

7. Follow the manufacturer's instructions to either:
   - A: Set the offset to –.600 MHz.
   - B: Set the radio's receive frequency to 146.325 MHz.
8. Press the PTT and say your call sign into the radio's microphone, then release the PTT.
9. If your settings are correct, and the repeater is in range of your radio, you should hear a beep, tone, or short static burst. You might also receive an answer from another ham radio operator!

USING A DIRECTIONAL OR GAIN ANTENNA

A vertical mag mount antenna, usually intended for a temporary mobile installation, but here, it's mounted to an HVAC ceiling vent for a makeshift base station. Right side up or upside down doesn't matter as long as the polarity is vertical.

Directional or gain antennas can drastically improve communication range compared to an omnidirectional antenna. All the personal radio services use AM or FM modulation, which primarily uses vertically polarized antennas. Standard vertical antennas are omnidirectional and emit radio waves equally in all directions horizontally. The signal weakens as the launch angle gets steeper. Visualized, it would look similar to a doughnut with the vertical antenna in the doughnut's hole.

A vertical antenna works well for contacting someone in an unknown location. You stand as much chance of making contact with someone 1 mile north of you as you do someone one mile south, assuming the surrounding terrain is flat and unobstructed.

Gain antennas, sometimes called directional antennas, don't increase the power of the radio but concentrate the signal in a general direction. Vertically polarized gain antennas intensify the signal horizontally. Visualizing this would look like "squishing" the previously mentioned doughnut so that it reaches farther from the center. Gain antennas are not permitted on FRS radios.

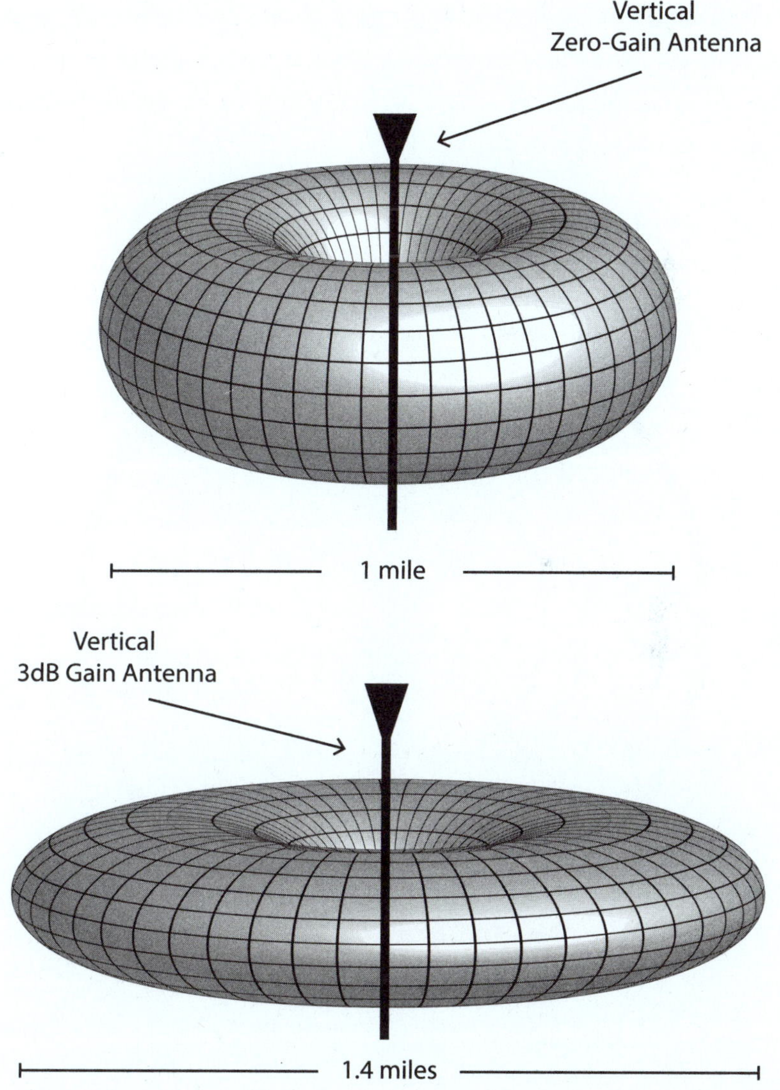

A zero-gain vertical antenna's doughnut-shaped (torus) pattern compared to a 3dB gain vertical antenna. Notice that the pattern is "squished" so that more power is directed horizontally and less vertically. 3dB gain is effectively twice the radiated power, which equals a 1.4 increase in distance. Doubling the distance requires four times the power or 6dB gain. Keep this in mind when considering the purchase of a gain antenna.

A horizontal gain antenna intensifies the signal in a particular compass direction and is most often used to increase SSB signals, which apply to CB and ham radio only. Yagi and Log Periodic antennas are the most common horizontal gain antennas. Mounting or holding a directional antenna vertically creates vertical polarity and maintains much of the increased signal strength in the direction the antenna is pointing. However, its effectiveness as an emergency communication antenna is questionable due to its directivity and attenuation of off-axis signals.

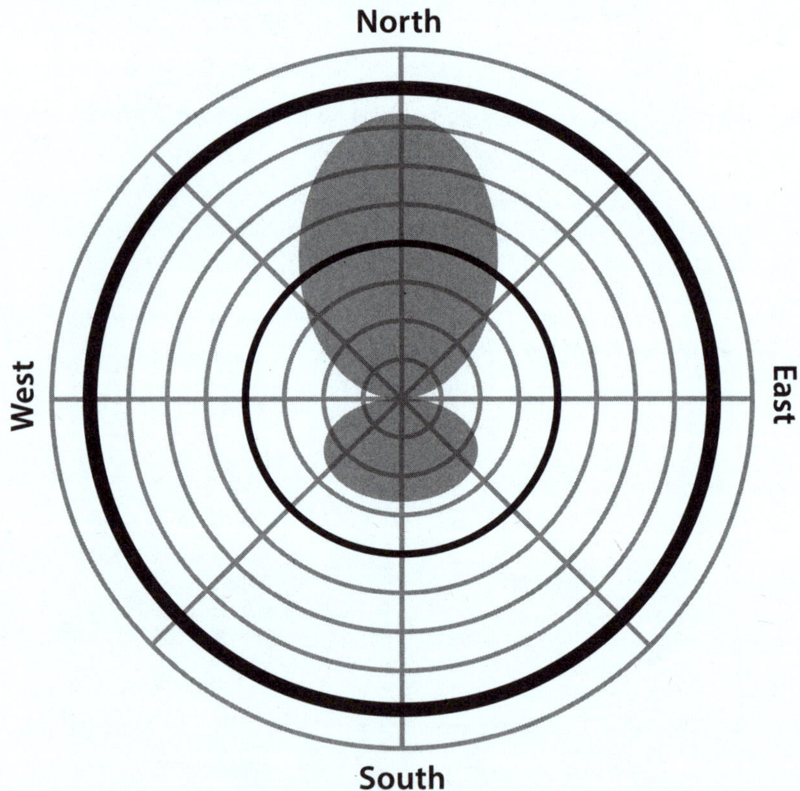

The transmission pattern of a directional antenna, such as a Yagi.

NVIS antennas are the horizontal antenna of choice for emergency and disaster HF radio communicators, but it's good for you to be aware of them if you pursue HF communication.

Some other antennas and their benefits are:

- J-pole
  - Vertical.
  - VHF/UHF.
  - The roll-up version is portable for go-kits or bug out bags.
  - Mildly directional but usually considered omnidirectional.
- Wire Dipole
  - Horizontal (most common) or vertical.
  - Horizontal is bidirectional from the sides of the antenna.
  - Vertical is omnidirectional.
  - Simplest and most common HF antenna.
  - Easy to build and operate.
  - Variations include half-wave dipole, off-center-fed, folded, and so on.
- Long Wire
  - Vertical, horizontal, or sloping.
  - Vertical is omnidirectional.
  - Horizontal is bidirectional.
  - Sloping is mildly directional.
  - Very basic antenna.
  - Moderately difficult to build and operate.
  - Very portable.
  - Variations include end-fed, random, Zepp, and so on.
- Full Wave Loops
  - Vertical or horizontal.
  - Complicated to construct.
  - Very quiet reception.
  - Some variations are directional.
  - Variations include delta, quad, cubical-quad, and so on.

Joe, one of the authors, uses a homemade Yagi directional antenna made from PVC and a tape measure. He's holding the elements vertically to connect a repeater that is just out of reach with the handheld's stock antenna.

OVERCOMING WEAK LINE-OF-SIGHT SIGNALS

Apart from excessive distance, the most common cause of a weak line-of-sight signal is antenna polarity. A horizontal antenna receives less than 5 percent of a signal transmitted from a vertical antenna. The fix is easy; make sure both antennas are held vertically. This isn't an issue between base and mobile antennas because they're permanently mounted vertically. However, if you're having trouble hearing another radio with your handheld, check to make sure the antenna is vertical.

Another common cause of weak line-of-sight signals is location. It's particularly true in urban settings, mountainous terrain, or canyons. The fix is often as simple as moving the antenna a few feet left or right or to a higher elevation.

Two-Way Radio Procedures and Tactics

This section will help you understand how to become a clear and effective radio communicator by teaching radio etiquette, communicator mindset, and strategies for clarity. Mastering basic operating procedures is the most effective way to overcome weak signals. Knowing what to say, when to say it, and how to say it is the most important aspect of emergency communication.

You've probably had trouble expressing yourself in a stressful situation. The stress is compounded when you can't rely on face-to-face visual cues. Emergency communication requires communicating with someone you can't see while one or both of you are under duress. Luckily, there are some basic procedures and practices you can follow to help.

USING THE PHONETIC ALPHABET

Unclear messages during a disaster have serious consequences. Learning how to spell things out clearly is an important skill for every operator. Using the phonetic alphabet to spell words is invaluable when words are difficult to understand. They also help distinguish between homophones such as there/their/they're or to/too/two. We'll discuss this further in the next section about pro words.

A Alpha	B Bravo	C Charlie	D Delta	E Echo
F Foxtrot	G Golf	H Hotel	I India	J Juliette
K Kilo	L Lima	M Mike	N November	O Oscar
P Papa	Q Quebec	R Romeo	S Sierra	T Tango
U Uniform	V Victor	W Whiskey	X X-ray	Y Yankee
Z Zulu				

PROCEDURE WORDS (PRO WORDS)

Procedure words, or pro words, are practical tools in radio communication. They are a shorthand form of communication that you'll most certainly encounter during disaster communications. Knowing these words not only saves time but also helps to make you a better communicator when time is of utmost importance. They help coordinate communication, prevent you from talking over each other, and ensure accurate information. Pro words are unnecessary for most repeater communication or radios that emit a courtesy tone or static burst when the PTT is released.

- EMERGENCY, EMERGENCY, EMERGENCY. Hopefully, this is the pro word you'll hear or use the least, but it's the most critical one. Saying "emergency" three times will capture everyone's attention and stop all nonemergency communication.
  - If you hear an EMERGENCY call for help, grab a pencil and paper and be ready to copy all information given, even if you're not the person answering. If you write down the information, you'll be prepared to provide a relay or fill in any information if the signal is lost between the other two stations.
  - If you are the person who responds to a call for help, make sure to get the what, when, where, and who (age, gender, and so on). Avoid giving or asking for full, proper names. First names are usually enough

information. (We'll talk about this more in the OPSEC section in Chapter 7.) Contact the appropriate first responders once you've collected all the necessary information.

- MAYDAY, MAYDAY, MAYDAY also indicates an emergency, but the word EMERGENCY is more universally understood.
- AFFIRMATIVE means "yes."
- NEGATIVE means "no."
- FIGURES is helpful when you're about to say a numeral as part of a sentence. For example, "Please send medical assistance to 220 Main Street." The homophones "to" and "2" in "200" might be confused in a stressful situation. The better practice is to say, "Please send medical assistance to FIGURES TWO TWO ZERO Main Street." FIGURES can also be used before reading any mixed group of alphanumeric characters that starts with a number. For example, 539NBC would be said, "FIGURES FIVE THREE NINER NOVEMBER BRAVO CHARLIE."
- I SPELL is handy when communicating homophones and uncommon spellings of proper nouns. The correct usage is to say the word, spell it phonetically, and say the word again, "The address is fifteen Maine, I SPELL MIKE ALPHA INDIA NOVEMBER ECHO, Maine Avenue." I SPELL is also used before a group of mixed alphanumeric characters that begin with a letter. WSGU968 would be spoken as, "I SPELL WHISKEY SIERRA GOLF UNIFORM NINER SIX EIGHT."
- INFORMATION is used to "break" into an ongoing conversation with valuable information directly related to the discussion. To use INFORMATION, wait for a break in the conversation, then push the PTT and say the word INFORMATION or INFO. Wait for a station to acknowledge you and then share your information. INFORMATION is also known as a BREAKTAG.
- QUERY is related to INFORMATION, but it is used to ask for information about the discussed topic. Wait for a break in the conversation, push the PTT button, then say QUERY. When you're acknowledged, ask your question.
- OVER is the most often used pro word. Some radios and repeaters emit a "courtesy tone" or other indicator to let you know that the PTT has been

released, but if not, use OVER just before releasing the PTT to let the other person know that it's their turn to talk.

- OUT indicates the end of the conversation. Despite what we've seen in the movies, OVER and OUT are never used together. Saying OVER AND OUT is like saying, "I'm done with my thought; it's your turn to talk, but the conversation is over." Saying OUT lets everyone on the frequency know you're done communicating and it is available.
- OUT TO YOU is similar to OUT but only concludes communication with the other station. It indicates that you are still using the frequency and intend to call a different station immediately.
- ROGER lets the other station know you understand what they said. It might also be used to indicate "I agree."
- STANDBY or WAIT indicates that you'll release your PTT momentarily but will begin transmitting after a brief pause.
- WILCO means that you will do or comply with a request or instruction. Despite what they do in the movies, ROGER-WILCO is never used because it's redundant. Agreeing to follow an instruction implies that we understand it.

Traffic or Message Precedence

You will need to give your message a proper level of urgency so that they get through in the order you intend. Precedence usually applies to formal written messages, sometimes called "record traffic." The precedence indicates how urgent the message is.

- EMERGENCY traffic is *always* sent or addressed first. The precedence EMERGENCY differs from the pro word EMERGENCY in that it doesn't indicate that the person saying it is in imminent danger. This author has never heard the precedence EMERGENCY used. *Don't use this precedence if you have any doubt that an emergency exists.*
- PRIORITY is used for any message that needs to be acted on or delivered within a specific time frame, usually less than 24 hours. PRIORITY messages are always handled first.

- WELFARE traffic is either a request or information about the welfare of an individual in an area affected by a disaster. WELFARE messages are addressed only after all EMERGENCY and PRIORITY traffic is cleared.
- ROUTINE is the most common traffic and is handled last.

Q Codes

Q Codes are very important for any disaster communicator to know and can be a powerful communication tool. They are primarily used for ham radio Morse code communication, but you may encounter them in voice communication. This book won't do a deep dive into them, but it's good for you to be familiar with the most common ones. Q Codes are used *only* with ham radio.

- CQ: Used to request contact with any station.
- QSL: Understood. It's sometimes used as both a question and answer to assure that the message was understood, "I'm on my way home. QSL?" - "QSL"
- QSO: A conversation.
- QRM: Human-made interference, either accidental or intentional.
- QRN: Natural interference, such as static from lightning.
- QTH: Your location.

10 Codes

It's important to understand when, and when not, to use 10 Codes. 10 Codes are popular with CBers and are occasionally used on other personal radio services, except ham radio. 10 Codes are *never* appropriate on ham radio frequencies. The most well known are 10-4 for "yes" and 10-20 for "location." Note: Secret codes, hidden meanings, and encryption are illegal on all personal radio services. While there are dozens of 10 Codes, some of the most popular are:

- 10-1 = Receiving poorly.
- 10-2 = Receiving well.
- 10-3 = Stop transmitting.
- 10-4 = Message received.

- 10-5 = Relay message to ______.
- 10-6 = Busy, please stand by.
- 10-7 = Out of service, leaving the air.
- 10-8 = In service, subject to call.

Quick Action Checklist

Use the checklist that follows to evaluate your current knowledge in radio communication basics and identify areas where you may need further practice or study.

❑ Do you know what to say and what not to say during a radio transmission?

❑ Is it your nature to remain calm during times of stress (if not, don't worry, we cover tips for this in Chapter 12)?

❑ Do you have the entire NATO phonetic alphabet memorized?

❑ Have you practiced spelling out names and locations to your team members using this alphabet?

❑ Do you know the proper function of each pro word?

❑ Can you decipher common Q Codes or 10 Codes if you hear them?

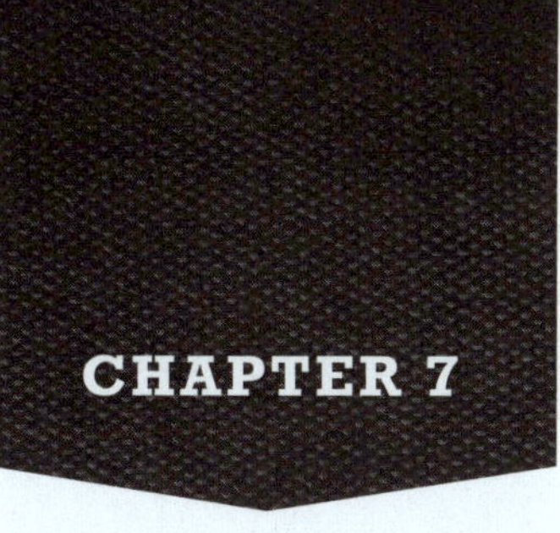

HOW TO MAKE CONTACT

In this chapter, you will learn how to make contact, request and give signal reports, and more to make clear communication. This chapter will prepare you to be an effective disaster communicator whether communicating with family members nearby or with disaster personnel long-range. You'll take a practical look at how to be a competent two-way radio communicator. And you'll learn the meat of communicating: how to make contact between radios, what to say, how to say it, and when to say it, including operational security (OPSEC) and situational awareness.

How to Make Contact

One of the core skills of radio communication is what's called "making contact." Whether you're reaching out to a friend or stranger, this section will help you understand the proper step-by-step process for making contact correctly.

CONTACTING A KNOWN STATION

Making radio contact with someone you know is a straightforward process. Following is the process for making this clear and legal.

1. Tune to a predetermined frequency.
2. Set a predetermined privacy tone.
3. Listen for a few minutes to see if the frequency is in use.

4. If nothing is heard, hold the microphone about four fingers away from your mouth, push the PTT, wait about one second, and then ask, "Is this frequency in use?" (Don't forget to say your call sign for GMRS or ham radio.)
5. If no one answers, continue to the next step. If the frequency is in use, try a different frequency.
6. Hold the microphone about four fingers away from your mouth.
7. Press the PTT and wait about one second before speaking.
8. Announce the name, handle, or call sign (depending on the radio service's rules) of the other station and then your own. (It's good to repeat the call if the other station isn't expecting to hear from you.)
   - Ham radio example: "KK4ECR this is W1WCN, KK4ECR this is W1WCN, OVER."
   - GMRS example: "Scott, this is Joe, Scott, this is Joe, WSGU948, OVER."
   - FRS doesn't require a call sign.
   - *Always* announce the other person's name or call sign first. This assures their ears are "turned on" to hear who is calling.
9. The other station answers, "Joe, this is Scott, OVER."
10. Conduct the conversation.

CONTACTING AN UNKNOWN STATION

Sometimes, it's necessary to contact anyone who might hear you. The process is similar to contacting a known station, whether you want to make a new friend, see who might be on frequency, get a signal report, or ask for help.

"Calling" frequencies are a good place to make a random contact. GMRS/FRS and ham radio have specific frequencies for "calling." CB radio doesn't have "calling" frequencies but does have frequencies commonly used for specific purposes, such as Channel 19, which is popular with truckers and travelers. MURS doesn't have a calling frequency.

- GMRS/FRS: 462.675 MHz (Channel 20)
- Ham radio: VHF 146.520 MHz, UHF 446.000 MHz

Making contact through a local GMRS or ham radio repeater is also common. You can find repeater information at www.repeaterbook.com and https://myGMRS.com.

The process for contacting an unknown station is similar to contacting a known station.

1. Tune to a calling or repeater frequency.
2. Turn off PL tones if using a calling frequency; set the appropriate PL tone if using a repeater.
3. Listen for a few minutes to see if the frequency is in use.
4. If nothing is heard, hold the microphone about four fingers away from your mouth, push the PTT, wait about one second, and then ask, "Is this frequency in use?" (Don't forget to say your call sign for GMRS or ham radio.)
5. If no one answers, continue to the next step. If the frequency is in use, see step 10.*
6. Hold the microphone about four fingers away from your mouth.
7. Press the PTT and wait about one second before speaking.
   - Waiting before speaking is particularly important because some repeaters have a slight delay. Starting to speak too soon after pushing the PTT may cut off the beginning of your transmission.
8. Here are some phrases to use to make a random contact:
   - "This is [your call sign or ID], is anyone on frequency?"
   - "This is [your call sign or ID] requesting a radio check."
   - "This is [your call sign or ID] seeking to make a contact."
9. Wait a few seconds to see if someone replies. Repeating your request is okay if someone doesn't answer the first time.
10. If someone answers, enjoy the conversation. *If someone is having a conversation on the repeater, it's acceptable to ask to join the conversation if you so desire.
11. Wait for a break in the conversation.
12. Hold the microphone about four fingers away from your mouth.
13. Press the PTT, say your call sign once, then release the PTT.
14. Wait for one of the others to acknowledge you.

15. If they don't answer, wait for another break and try again. If they don't respond after a third attempt, the conversation might not be open for you to join.
16. If they answer, enjoy the conversation.

Radio Checks and Signal Reports

Radio checks and signal reports are the best way to test your radio gear. Testing your gear is essential. You will need to know how to request and understand signal reports so that problems can be identified before they happen. The process is simple.

1. Tune to a calling or repeater frequency.
2. Set PL tones, if necessary.
3. Listen for a few minutes to see if the frequency is in use.
4. As always, ask if the frequency is in use.
5. If nothing is heard, hold the microphone about four fingers away from your mouth, push the PTT, wait about one second, and then say, "This is [your call sign or ID] requesting a radio check."
6. You may hear one of the following reports. For FM or repeater operation:
   - "Full quieting" or "Loud and clear"—No static, good audio.
   - "Hitting the repeater"—The repeater is activating, but there might be issues such as low audio, distortion, static, and so on. The other station will probably give further information.
   - "Unable to copy" or "No Copy"—Something is severely wrong with the signal, i.e., too weak, severely distorted, and so on. Remember that there are two "hops" when using a repeater: your signal to the repeater and the repeater's signal to the other radio. The problem might not be with your signal; it could be an issue between the repeater and the other station.
   - If someone is kind enough to provide a signal report, it's good manners to give one back: "You're loud and clear too."
7. You may hear one of the following reports. For AM or SSB voice transmissions:

- A two-digit numerical rating system for AM and SSB transmission is customary for AM or SSB radio checks. The first number is a 1–5 rating for "readability" or how much is understood.
    - 5: Hearing all words clearly.
    - 4: Hearing most words but need to listen carefully.
    - 3: Difficult to hear all words.
    - 2: Understanding less than half of the words.
    - 1: Unreadable.
- The radio's meter indicates the second number (1–9). It is possible to have a signal above 9, which would be "Plus 10, plus 20, and so on" depending on what the meter indicates.
- The signal report is given as two distinct numbers, such as 5-9 or 4-3, instead of "59" or "43."
- Here are some sample responses:
    - 5-9 indicates "loud and clear."
    - 4-5 indicates "weak, but readable."

An analog S-meter (many are now digital). Notice the "S" left of the second arc from the top. A signal that's fully intelligible with the needle reaching S-7 will receive a signal report of "5-7." (The other arcs (Ip, HV, COMP, and ALC) are for advanced settings outside the scope of this book.)

Radio Nets

A radio net is an on-air meeting of radio operators with a shared purpose. This section will teach you how to create one or participate in one to help meet your disaster communication goals by forming organized groups of communicators. Most radio nets take place on ham frequencies, but they can be helpful in any radio service. There are two primary net formats: formal nets, also called directed nets, and informal nets.

Formal nets occur regularly on specific frequencies on specific dates, at specific times, except for emergency and disaster response nets, which take place as needed. Formal nets focus on various topics:

- Weather reports and related issues.
- Travel information.
- Information of shared interest, such as buying, selling, and trading radio gear and hobbies.
- Sending, relaying, and receiving written messages (traffic nets).
- Emergency operations and procedures training.
- Emergency response (called an emergency net).

Informal nets are like roundtable discussions without any clear emphasis. Topics run the gamut and might change at the whim of the participants. These are usually called "rag chew" nets. This chapter will concentrate on emergency nets and their supporting training nets.

The net control operator or station is responsible for facilitating net business, coordinating communication, and instructing how messages should be sent and received. On a directed net, stations may not contact each other directly without permission from the net control operator.

Formal nets begin with the announcement of a preamble, which outlines the purpose and procedures of the net. Part of the preamble asks for any stations with emergency or priority traffic (messages). After, or as part of, reading the preamble, the net control station will assign a backup net control station. Here is a sample preamble for a ham radio emergency training net, including check-in procedures.

"Attention, all stations. This is [call sign or ID]. I am in net control. Backup net control is [call sign or ID of backup]."

"Is there any station with emergency or priority traffic? Announce your call sign only, please."

[Release your PTT and listen for any stations.]

[Process any emergency or priority traffic accordingly, before proceeding. If none is heard, proceed with the preamble.]

"This net meets on this repeater every Sunday evening at 1930 local time. The backup repeater is the Main St. repeater."

"The purpose of this net is to increase the readiness of local radio operators and their equipment in the event of a communication emergency, and share information of interest to the radio community."

"This is a directed net; net control will direct all communications. All stations are encouraged to check in with us and pass traffic. The use of correct phonetics and adhering to normal net procedures is encouraged. When checking in, please speak slowly and give your call sign phonetically ONCE and ONCE ONLY, to ensure net control correctly acknowledges your call. When checking in to the net, advise net control if you have any relevant traffic, comments, or announcements. It is not necessary to advise net control that you have "NO TRAFFIC." Announcements, comments, and traffic will be handled after check-ins are complete."

[Use the pro word WAIT, then release your PTT to listen for a few seconds. If no one is attempting contact, continue with check-ins.]

"Nothing heard. We will now take general check-ins. This net takes check-ins in suffix order. Your suffix is the letters following the number in your call sign."

"Stations whose suffix begins with Alpha through Golf, Alpha through Golf, come with your full call sign now, please."

[Release PTT and listen for check-ins. Record each check-in on a log sheet. After several have checked in, push your PTT and repeat each back to acknowledge that you heard them.]

[Ask again for "Alpha through Golf" until no one else replies, then repeat the process for "Hotel through Oscar," and then, "Papa through Zulu."]

[After the last group of Papa through Zulu are acknowledged, ask for relays and missed stations.]

"This is net control, and my call sign is [call sign]. Are there any relays or stations not acknowledged by net control?"

[Once no more stations answer the "net calls," proceed with handling traffic and any net business or training.]

[Call for any late or missed check-ins after completing the net business and all messages have been sent.]

This is net control, and my call sign is [call sign]. Are there any late or missed check-ins? Come with your call sign now, please."

[Record these stations, then close the net.]

"This concludes all business for this net. Thank you to everyone who participated and assisted with relays and traffic. This is [call sign], securing the net at [current local time] and returning the frequency to normal amateur use. OUT."

This preamble is just a suggestion. Be as formal or informal as your group is comfortable.

POINTS TO CONSIDER

When thinking about your ability to make contact in an emergency situation, consider these questions:

- Can you confidently initiate a call to a known or unknown station?
- Have you practiced the script(s) to make contact with a known or unknown station?

- Do you understand how to request and provide a signal report?
- Would a radio net benefit your family, community, or team communication plan?
- Do you need your own net, or would it be better to join an existing net in your area?

Interference, Operational Security (OPSEC), and Situational Awareness

You need to keep your communication secure and safe by avoiding distractions, unscrupulous communicators, and accidental security leaks. Both natural and human-made interference can impede radio communication. Fortunately, natural interference rarely interferes with AM/FM line-of-sight radio signals, where most emergency communication occurs. Natural interference is much more common on the high frequencies of ham radio.

Human-made interference is much more troublesome in line-of-sight communication. The most common human interference is unintentional. Limited GMRS/FRS, MURS, and CB frequencies can cause channel overcrowding, particularly when people are desperate to make contact following a catastrophic event.

Believe it or not, some individuals will intentionally interfere with emergency communication. Unfortunately, intentional interference is more challenging to eliminate than unintentional interference, but there are ways it can be mitigated. First, let's look at using privacy tones to prevent unintentional interference.

PRIVACY TONES

Privacy tones can be used to filter out interference, but using them can give you a false sense of privacy. All personal radio services, except CB, allow privacy tones or privacy codes. Privacy tones are subaudible tones that are transmitted when the PTT is pushed. Radios with the same privacy tone hear each other. Radios with different privacy tones don't hear each other. A radio with *no* privacy tone will receive every signal on that frequency.

For example, in the following image, radio operators A, B, C, D, and E all use Channel 5. Radios A, B, and C use privacy tone 2; D and E use privacy tone 6. A, B, and C hear each other but can't hear D and E. D and E hear each other but can't hear A, B, and C. Radio user X is also tuned to Channel 5 with no privacy tone. User X can listen to everyone else, but none will hear him. Anyone within transmitting distance without a PL tone will hear operator X.

There are three common types of privacy tones:

- PL tone
- Continuous Tone Coded Squelch System (CTCSS)
- Digital Coded Squelch (DCS)

The most basic privacy tone is a simple PL tone that doesn't affect squelch. Remember, squelch mutes static and background noise a radio receives when there isn't a strong signal. The other two privacy tones, CTCSS and DCS, suppress squelch and inhibit interference.

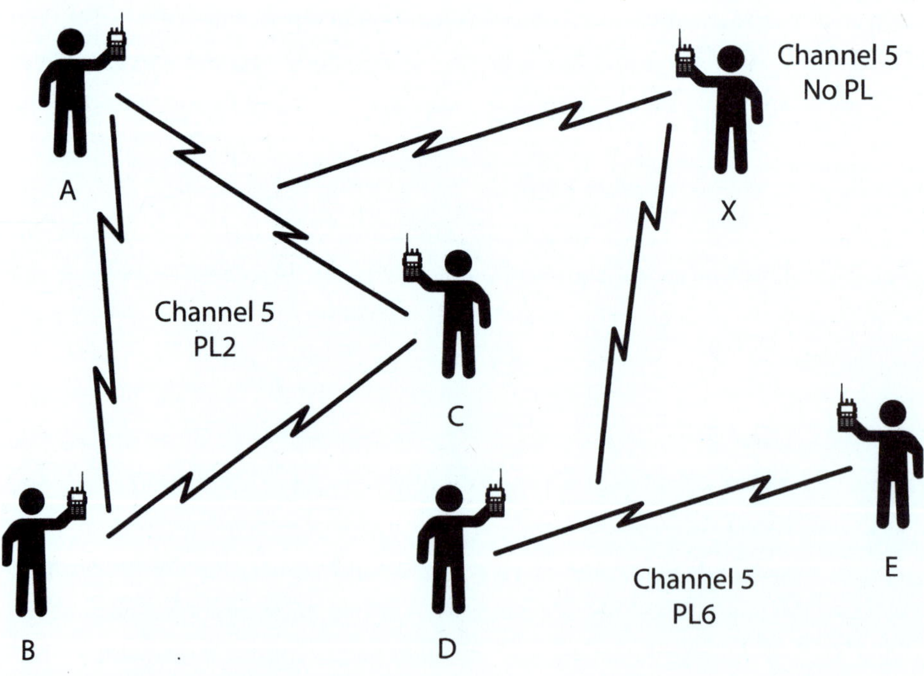

This image depicts the privacy tone scenario described.

Unfortunately, the term "privacy tone" is misleading. Privacy tones don't prevent other people from hearing your radio conversation; privacy tones prevent the other person's conversation from interfering with yours. Think of it this way: Hanging a "Privacy Please" card on the door of your hotel room doesn't mean that people won't be able to hear what's going on in your room, but it does mean that room service won't interrupt you. Counter-intuitively, *not* using a privacy tone provides more operational security than using one, but at the expense of increased interference.

INTENTIONAL INTERFERENCE

At times you may have to deal with intentional interference from unscrupulous communicators. Knowing how to react can save you time and hassle. As previously mentioned, some individuals will try to interfere with your communication intentionally. If it happens to you, *ignore it*!

This can't be emphasized enough. Don't mention it, don't refer to it, don't complain about it, and definitely don't engage or threaten the instigator. Doing so lets them know they're having an effect, which encourages them to continue. So, what should you do? Here are two strategies (we like to give malicious interferers the mock call sign ID1OT).

1. Continue communicating as if the interference isn't there. If ID1OT thinks you don't hear them, they'll stop. Remember that FRS, GMRS, MURS, and ham radio use FM transmissions. The strongest signal usually wins with FM. This is called the capture effect. Chances are good that you and your communication partner are closer to each other than ID1OT is to either of you, so the capture effect will work in your favor. You won't hear the interference when either of you transmits. Try boosting your power if the capture effect isn't working for you. If that still doesn't work, use strategy 2.
2. Switch to a predetermined frequency and/or privacy tone. It's good to have at least two backup frequencies that everyone in your group knows and in what order they should be used. For example, if you're operating on Channel 4 and unwanted signals interfere with your communication, everyone automatically switches to Channel 6. If that frequency

is occupied, or ID1OT happens to find you there, switch to Channel 12. Using different privacy tones on each channel is even better. This strategy works best when you don't announce that you're switching frequencies on the air, so be sure to include them in your personal communication plan. That way, everyone knows, "If the first channel is unusable, switch to the second channel. If that channel isn't available, switch to the third."

OPERATIONAL SECURITY (OPSEC) AND COMMUNICATIONS SECURITY (COMSEC)

You will need to protect your personal data while communicating over public frequencies. Operational security (OPSEC) keeps information from people who might use it to harm you or others. Communications security (COMSEC) ensures that confidential information stays confidential during communication.

Remember, your two-way communication occurs on open frequencies. Anyone with a radio or scanner on your frequency can hear everything you say. Secret codes, hidden meanings, and encryption are forbidden on personal radio services, so you must protect the data you share through two-way radio. You can do this by 1) thinking through, even writing down, what you want to say before you push the PTT button and start talking, and 2) being brief and concise with your messages. A good rule is, "The less you say, the less you divulge."

Here's a list of things to avoid communicating on the air, even in casual conversation:

- Full names
- Mailing addresses
- Phone numbers
- Travel plans (vacation, long weekends, and so on)
- Work schedule
- Medical information (HIPAA regulations apply)
- Financial information
- Driver's license and/or Social Security numbers

It's sometimes beneficial to use "tactical" call signs or IDs. Tactical call signs identify a station by location or function rather than the individual. This eliminates confusion and streamlines communication when two or more operators share a responsibility.

For example, three operators with different call signs are rotating responsibility at the county's special needs emergency shelter, which has been assigned the tactical call sign "SPECIAL NEEDS." It's much easier for another station to call "SPECIAL NEEDS" than to try and remember which individual, and their call sign, is on duty at that particular time. Remember, though, that individual FCC-issued call signs must still be used at the end of the transmissions.

Finally, the digital modes available on ham and GMRS radios add a layer of privacy. While digital communication can't be encrypted, intercepting digital information is more difficult than voice communication. Bad actors are lazy opportunists who will avoid the extra work to decode digital signals.

POINTS TO CONSIDER

When thinking about privacy, consider these points:

- Are you sharing personal information during your practice communications?
- Do you understand the importance of establishing backup channels or frequencies in case security is compromised?
- Are you protecting information about specific plans and locations?

Intelligence Collection and Situational Awareness

An important aspect of radio communication is gathering information, also known as intelligence collection, to make informed decisions. Evaluating and using that information to know what's happening around you is called situational awareness. Radios are potent tools for gathering open-source intelligence (OSINT) and communication intelligence (COMINT). OSINT is collected by monitoring public information, such as broadcast radio. You can gather COMINT by listening to two-way radio communication.

In the following sections, you'll find a variety of resources to gather OSINT and COMINT. These are important because they can keep you informed when some of your typical sources, like the Internet, are unavailable. As you review these resources, decide which seem important enough for you to add to your own communication toolbox.

BROADCAST RADIO AND THE EMERGENCY ALERT SYSTEM (EAS)

Commercial broadcast radio stations transmit in either FM or AM and provide valuable information before, during, and after disasters. They do this as part of the Emergency Alert System (EAS), a national public warning system. Federal, state, and local officials use the EAS to share weather warnings, AMBER alerts, and large-scale threats to life and property.

An old-school transistor radio is the easiest way to receive EAS messages. You may already have one lying around the house, or you can find a basic one for $10–$15. It doesn't need to be fancy. All it needs is an on/off volume and a tuning knob. Every hurricane kit, bug in box, and winter car kit should have one.

THE NOAA WEATHER RADIO ALL HAZARDS (NWR)

NOAA Weather Radio broadcasts weather information twenty-four hours a day, seven days a week. The broadcasts come directly from the National Weather Service (NWS) office and are broadcast on seven specifically allocated frequencies in the VHF range. Most NOAA radios automatically scan for or are preprogrammed with these frequencies. NWR stations exist in all fifty states, the US Virgin Islands, and the US Pacific territories. Each station has a transmission range of 40–50 miles.

Most EAS alerts are weather-related, but the EAS also reports nonweather-related disasters like earthquakes, tsunamis, landslides, insect infestations, terrorist attacks, and so on. The NWS runs an alert test at least once weekly, usually on Wednesdays between 10:00 AM and noon local time. NOAA radio frequencies are: 162.400 MHz, 162.425 MHz, 162.450 MHz, 162.475 MHz, 162.500 MHz, 162.525 MHz, and 162.550 MHz.

SCANNERS

Commonly called police scanners, these radios allow you to monitor multiple frequencies. Scanners can scan all the frequencies in a particular range or a series of preselected channels where valuable communication is known to occur. The scanner stops scanning whenever it hears a signal. It will start scanning again after some time or stay on that frequency until the signal stops before it resumes scanning.

Scanners can monitor police, fire and rescue, marine, aeronautical, and utilities. Listening to these services is legal in all fifty states and US territories, but using a scanner in your car in some states is illegal. Check your state and local laws before scanning first responder frequencies. It's common for radio enthusiasts to scan local sheriff and fire rescue frequencies, especially during severe weather. (RadioReference.com is an excellent resource for finding local frequencies.)

UNITED STATES COAST GUARD (USCG) MARINE VHF

Monitoring information from large bodies of water and waterways can provide insight into conditions during a disaster. The United States Coast Guard (USCG) regularly broadcasts weather updates and warnings on marine VHF frequencies. They also broadcast navigation, water hazards, and other urgent safety information. Channel 16 (156.800 MHz) is the marine distress channel and calling frequency. The USCG continuously monitors it. Channel 1022 (157.100 MHz) is the marine VHF information and safety channel. (Channel 1022 was 22a before 2023.)

SHORTWAVE BROADCAST RADIO STATIONS

Shortwave radio is a one-way, one-to-many global communication medium with valuable information from hundreds or thousands of miles away. Shortwave broadcasts will certainly be resurgent in a global crisis. Most recently, the BBC increased its shortwave presence after Russia invaded Ukraine. Shortwave broadcast schedules can be found at www.short-wave.info.

RADIO STATIONS WWV AND WWVH

WWV and WWVH are shortwave radio stations that transmit a time signal twenty-four hours a day, seven days a week, on frequencies 2.500, 5.000, 10.000, and 15.000 MHz; WWV also broadcasts on frequency 20.000 MHz, but WWVH does not. The WWV/WWVH stations also transmit valuable information during a large-scale communication infrastructure outage.

UNITED STATES COAST GUARD HF AND RADIOFAX WEATHER BROADCASTS

The USCG also broadcasts voice and weather map information on HF. A computer or smart device can capture weather charts and satellite images with a shortwave radio capable of upper sideband reception. USCG Radiofax information can be found at www.weather.gov/marine/uscg_broadcasts.

AIR TRAFFIC CONTROL (ATC)

A lot of valuable information can be gleaned from aircraft communication. Local airport ATC frequencies can be found at RadioReference.com. You can also scan 118.00–135.975 for aviation communication in your area.

VOLMET

VOLMET HF broadcasts provide weather information to inflight aircraft twenty-four hours a day, seven days a week. The Earth is divided into regions, and several VOLMET transmitters serve each area to ensure complete coverage. VOLMET transmissions are automated and include weather information specific to each region. VOLMET frequencies can be found at https://wiki.radioreference.com/index.php/VOLMET.

LOCAL UTILITIES AND MEDICAL SERVICES

Knowing the progress of power restoration, water availability, and hospital status in your area provides peace of mind. Utility and business radio frequencies for your area can be found at RadioReference.com.

Next Steps to Improve As an Emergency/Disaster Radio Operator

As you dive into the world of radio communication, you'll likely want to grow your skills. Here are some organizations to connect with like-minded preparedness enthusiasts, develop emergency/disaster communication skills, and contribute to your local community.

- **Amateur Radio Emergency Service (ARES):** ARES is the primary ham radio emergency/disaster radio service. ARES' parent organization is the American Radio Relay League (ARRL), representing ham radio's interests in the United States. ARES members are well-trained volunteers who provide public service communication to both government and nongovernment organizations at the county, state, and national levels. Information about ARES can be found at www.arrl.org/ares.
- **AuxComm, USA:** The AuxComm, USA, organization supports local, state, and federal agencies with trained CB, GMRS, and ham radio operators. AuxComm, USA, shouldn't be confused with AUXCOMM (see later in this list). More information about AuxComm, USA, is available at www.auxcommusa.org.
- **AUXCOMM:** AUXCOMM is a backup communication system FEMA uses to support disaster recovery efforts. It utilizes several communication organizations, including training and certifications for ham, GMRS, CB, and other radio operators. Information can be found by searching the Internet for "AUXCOMM" in your state.
- **Hurricane Watch Net (HWN):** The Hurricane Watch Net is a ham radio organization that relays weather conditions in areas in the path of hurricanes to the National Hurricane Center in Miami, Florida. HWN members also provide emergency communication transmitted out of areas affected by hurricanes. They operate on frequencies 14.325 and 7.268 MHz. The Hurricane Watch Net website is at www.hwn.org.
- **Military Auxiliary Radio System (MARS):** MARS provides contingency communication services when conventional systems, like phone, cell, and Internet are unavailable or disrupted by complex catastrophes or cyberattacks. It's a civilian volunteer organization sponsored by the Department of Defense. MARS members must hold a valid ham radio license but operate on military frequencies, mainly in the HF range. Information can be found at www.usarmymars.org/home and https://community.apan.org/wg/afmars.
- **Radio Emergency Associated Communications Teams (REACT) International, Inc.:** REACT started as a CB Channel 9 monitoring organization. Now, they use FRS, GMRS, MURS, and other radio services to

provide communication services in the aftermath of disasters. You can find a REACT team near you at https://reactintl.org/team-locator.php.

- **Radio Amateur Civil Emergency Service (RACES):** RACES members are licensed ham radio operators who provide emergency communication for local and state government organizations when communication infrastructure fails.
- **Salvation Army Team Emergency Radio Network (SATERN):** SATERN supports The Salvation Army's ministry and relief efforts in the aftermath of disasters. SATERN ham radio operators provide contingency radio communication for The Salvation Army's local, divisional, and territorial command centers and headquarters. They also coordinate with the Hurricane Watch Net to relay "health and welfare" messages from areas affected by hurricanes and other natural disasters. Information can be found at www.salvationarmyusa.org/satern-program.
- **SKYWARN:** SKYWARN is a network of trained weather observers who provide information to the National Weather Service. SKYWARN isn't strictly a radio organization, but many SKYWARN members are also GMRS, CB, and/or ham radio operators who share eyewitness weather information and damage reports by radio. See www.weather.gov/skywarn for more information.

Quick Action Checklist

By now, you have a solid grasp on the foundational basics of emergency radio communications. Two-way radios are powerful tools, but only when combined with the skills to use them. You've learned how to make contact, navigate interference, extend range, and connect to repeaters. You've also learned how to make communications short, effective, and secure. This knowledge forms the backbone of disaster communications.

Using the information provided in this chapter, it's now time to make some decisions about which of the basic radio skills you need to study further and practice. Use the quick action checklist that follows to decide which of these makes the most sense for you and your circumstances.

How to Make Contact

- ❑ Contacting a known station
- ❑ Contacting an unknown station
- ❑ Radio checks and signal reports
- ❑ Interference, OPSEC, and situational awareness
- ❑ Privacy tones
- ❑ How to deal with intentional interference
- ❑ Operational security (OPSEC) and communications security (COMSEC)

Intelligence Collection and Situational Awareness

- ❑ Emergency Alert System (EAS)
- ❑ National Oceanic and Atmospheric Administration (NOAA) Weather Radio All Hazards broadcasts
- ❑ Local police, fire and rescue, marine, aeronautical, and utility messages
- ❑ Shortwave global radio updates and messages
- ❑ WWV and WWVH radio stations
- ❑ United States Coast Guard HF and Radiofax weather broadcasts
- ❑ VOLMET HF broadcasts

Next Steps to Improve As an Emergency/Disaster Radio Operator

- ❑ ARES
- ❑ AuxComm, USA
- ❑ AUXCOMM
- ❑ Hurricane Watch Net
- ❑ MARS
- ❑ REACT
- ❑ RACES
- ❑ SATERN
- ❑ SKYWARN

PART 3

DIGITAL AND SATELLITE COMMUNICATION

In today's modern world, digital and satellite communication tools and systems provide an impressive array of solutions for staying connected in ways that even traditional off-grid communication tools fall short. And, in many instances, these tools make long-distance communication easier.

Whether through accessing Wi-Fi, leveraging mesh networks, or utilizing satellite tools for global coverage, the sky seems to no longer be the limit for what is possible. From Wi-Fi extenders and mobile hot spots to satellite phones and GPS texting devices, these tools offer reliable ways to message within a disaster zone, share critical information to those outside the disaster zone, and even coordinate rescue efforts.

In this part, you will learn about the most common and accessible digital and satellite communication tools, as well as the pros, cons, costs, and subscription plans for each. You'll learn how these tools are best integrated into and layered onto your traditional radio comms plan. And you'll understand the role these tools have played in more recent disasters and what that means for your own future of emergency communications.

Digital and satellite communications can be yet another layer of your emergency preparedness plan. Whether staying informed or signaling for help from areas cut off from communication, the information in this part ensures you have the tools to maintain connection when it matters most.

CHAPTER 8

DIGITAL COMMUNICATION TOOLS AND METHODS

It's common for large-scale disasters like hurricanes, wildfires, and earthquakes to take out landline phones, cell, and Internet services for entire communities, geographic areas, or multistate regions. This has a crippling effect on communication. Understanding how to use digital tools in those circumstances can help you stay connected, access updates, and share information. This chapter will give you some strategies to leverage computer and smart device interconnectivity to communicate with family and friends following a disaster.

Using and Maximizing Cellular, Internet, and Wi-Fi Access in a Disaster

What can you do if you don't have any cell, landline, or Internet service? In this case, there's not much you can do to access the outside world through the Internet, but just because the Internet is "out" doesn't mean that your home network isn't operating. Your home's Wi-Fi router is still a powerful communication tool for internal communication. Knowing how to squeeze every bit of functionality from an available network could give you the advantage you need in a grid-down disaster. This section will discuss some strategies for maximizing what is still working.

WI-FI EXTENDERS

Even when the Internet is down, a Wi-Fi extender can ensure you have network coverage across your immediate area or bug in location. You can extend the range of your Wi-Fi signal with a Wi-Fi extender, sometimes called a Wi-Fi repeater. As the name implies, a Wi-Fi extender *extends* the coverage of your Wi-Fi router's signal by repeating or rebroadcasting it.

Adding extenders to your network has some downsides, though. First, extenders can degrade the system's performance, slowing down data throughput. Second, each extender must be within range of the main router. This limits how large the coverage area can be. Finally, each extender broadcasts its own Service Set Identifier (SSID) or network name, which can lead to confusion when trying to connect a device as the signal is passed from one "node" area to another.

WI-FI MESH NETWORKS

If you need more robust Wi-Fi coverage for a larger home or group environment, you can try setting up a mesh network. Wi-Fi mesh networks are similar to Wi-Fi extenders, but rather than rebroadcasting the main router's signal, each mesh hub broadcasts its own Wi-Fi network. The hubs connect to and communicate with each other through a specific network connection called a "dedicated backhaul." This reserves bandwidth for your connected devices, which improves overall speed.

Mesh networks usually cover more square feet (up to 10,000) than extenders can. Another significant advantage of a mesh network is that the hubs all use the same SSID. Your connected devices see the mesh as one large Wi-Fi network. Connecting to different hubs is transparent to the end user. The downside is that mesh networks are usually more expensive than extenders.

WIDE-AREA MESH NETWORKS

Wide-area mesh networks allow an even broader area, or a larger community, to stay connected even when traditional infrastructure is offline. Wide-area mesh technology is like a home Wi-Fi mesh network on steroids. Coverage is measured in miles rather than feet. Entire communities can be interconnected without Internet service.

Wide-area mesh networks are peer-to-peer networks that directly connect devices (smartphones, tablets, radio transceivers, and so on) to each other. The devices act as nodes relaying data from device to device. The data might make several "hops" between devices before making it to the destination. Some wide-area mesh technology provides cellular voice communication, while others are limited to text only, and most use proprietary apps for setup and messaging.

There are several cost-effective, open-source mesh technologies, such as Meshtastic and LibreMesh. Meshtastic is easier to set up for family, local community, or ad hoc use. LibreMesh is more robust and scalable. A wide-area mesh network can serve as an "off-the-grid Internet" for preparation-minded families who want to communicate with each other between neighborhoods, subdivisions, or across town.

POINTS TO CONSIDER

When thinking about how best to utilize your Internet and Wi-Fi access during a power outage, consider these points:

- Do you have a way to power you home router and devices during a blackout (see Chapter 3)?
- Do you know how to use your home network with no Internet (local sharing, LAN communication, offline apps, etc.)?
- Have you mapped your Wi-Fi signal to determine if it's strong enough to reach your entire property or shelter area?
- Do you see value in adding a mesh network to help with internal family communication during a power/Internet outage?
- Do you know how to switch between Wi-Fi extenders if necessary?
- Do you have friends, family, or a close network of neighbors nearby who might be interested in forming a node-based network?
- Have you explored easy-entry mesh tools like Meshtastic?

If You Have Cell Service but No Internet

Even a weak cell phone signal can provide a lifeline of communication options. If you're lucky enough to have cell service following a disaster, the cell signals will be weak. The good news is texting doesn't require as strong or robust a signal as voice calls, so that's your best bet for getting in touch with family and friends outside the affected area.

You can scale up your data communication with a mobile hot spot. There are stand-alone hot spot devices, and many phones have a hot spot feature. They work by creating an ad hoc Wi-Fi network that connects to cell towers. The "weak signal data is better than voice" rule still applies here, but don't expect online gaming speed. Of course, performance will be degraded if several devices are connected to the hot spot. Most smartphones have hot spot capability, but stand-alone hot spots are the best option.

AUTOMATIC PACKET REPORTING SYSTEM (APRS)

Automatic Packet Reporting System (APRS) lets you automatically transmit your location and messages even when voice communication fails. It is a quasi-mesh system used by ham radio operators for real-time digital communication. GPS coordinates, weather information, and short text messages can be sent through a network of radios and "digipeaters." (Digipeaters are similar to the radio repeaters discussed earlier in this book, but they retransmit digital messages rather than voice.)

A mobile or portable APRS transmitter with GPS capability can be programmed to automatically transmit, or "beacon," the user's call sign, coordinates, and other data at preselected intervals. This data is received and decoded by radios at operation centers or base camps that can track the field operative's progress. Should voice contact with the field be lost, rescue or assistance teams can be dispatched to the field unit's last known location.

EMAIL IN EMERGENCIES

Email can be a powerful communication tool, even if voice communications aren't possible. If you're lucky enough to have Wi-Fi access or an Internet uplink such as cellular data or a satellite phone (discussed later), email communication via cell phone, tablet, or computer offers many advantages. These include:

- **Conservation:** Emails allow you to send messages to multiple people at once instead of making individual calls or texts. This not only conserves power but also reduces the bandwidth consumption of critical systems like cellular networks.
- **Attachments and complex messaging:** Unlike two-way radios or simple text messages, emails enable the sending of maps, pictures, and documents. The ability to share detailed and complex information drastically reduces radio usage and enhances coordination.
- **Multitasking:** Email allows you to send and receive messages while performing other tasks, unlike two-way radio communication, which often requires your full attention. This flexibility can significantly improve efficiency during disaster situations.
- **Global reach:** Email provides instantaneous global communication, whereas many other tools, like radios or local networks, have limited regional or local range.
- **Privacy:** Unlike many two-way radios, email is a more secure and private method for transmitting sensitive details such as addresses or medical information.

POINTS TO CONSIDER

When thinking of how you will communicate if you have cell service but no Internet, consider these questions:

- Have you communicated to everyone in your family or group that texting is better than calling in low-signal and/or emergency conditions?
- Have you enabled and tested the mobile hot spot feature on your phone by pairing it with a tablet or laptop?
- Do you see value in having a dedicated hot spot for emergencies?
- Does using APRS make sense for your communication goals?
- Do you see a benefit in your family, team, or group being able to send emails?

Ham Radio Digital Communication

When most people think of ham radio communication during a disaster, they might picture operators holding two-way radios and exchanging short, crude phrases. The reality is that many operators are seated at laptops, conducting what feels like business as usual—sending emails and accessing Internet resources. This is made possible not only by nearby power sources like generators, but also through the use of communication-specific software such as Winlink or local mesh networks.

Ham radio digital communication allows for silent sharing of information (such as files, email, and messages) when voice communication isn't possible or isn't enough. Ham radio operators can transmit and receive photos, email, text, and even interact with social media without direct connection to cell phones or the Internet. All of this is done with a personal computer or smart device connected to a ham radio through an audio or a digital interface.

The downside of digital communication is that adding components to the signal flow increases the number of failure points. There are relatively few failure points for voice communication: microphone/speaker-radio-antenna system. Adding a computer and all the parts that go with it increases the things that can go wrong and the amount of gear you have to carry to go portable.

POINTS TO CONSIDER

When thinking about getting involved with ham digital communication, consider these points:

- Are you, or do you desire to be, licensed to use ham digital modes?
- Do you need to send large batches of data?
- Do you have an aptitude for electrical devices, signal flow, and computers?
- Does additional gear align with your budget?

HOW HAM DIGITAL MODES WORK

Knowing how ham digital modes work will help you troubleshoot and choose the right modes for your needs, thus improving communication performance in critical moments.

Software

- Most ham radio digital software is open-source or freeware. The majority is Windows compatible, but there are Apple OS and Linux versions available. Some software can encode/decode various modes, but some software is mode specific.
- The best modes for emergency communication:
    - Packet Radio is well suited for sending text files and attachments. It is capable of both peer-to-peer and store-and-forward (email) communication.
    - MT63 can be used on HF, VHF, and UHF. It's a very robust mode that works well in poor conditions or through interference. It's primarily a real-time keyboard-to-keyboard communication tool.
    - PSK31 is a real-time keyboard-to-keyboard mode that works well when output power is limited. It has a comparatively low data rate, making for slow interchanges, but it more than compensates with excellent performance when other modes might fail.

Software and Apps

- FLDIGI is an open-source app that supports a wide variety of digital modes, including MT63, PSK31, and Radiofax (mentioned in Chapter 7).
- Narrow Band Emergency Messaging System (NBEMS) is an open-source software suite built around FLDIGI. As the name implies, it was developed specifically for emergency communications.
- Digital Master 780 (DM-780) is a sophisticated application that is part of the larger Ham Radio Deluxe suite that includes rig control and logging. DM-780 supports a wide array of digital modes. Ham Radio Deluxe is a pay-for application.
- Winlink Global Radio Email.

Hardware

- Windows, Apple OS, Linux (including Raspberry Pi OS) compatible computer or smart device.

- Audio or digital interface.
    - RIGblaster, SignaLink USB, terminal node controller (TNC).
    - Some radios have an internal audio or digital device.
- Computer controllable (tuning, PTT, etc.) ham radio.
    - Most ham radios can be connected to a computer through a USB or serial port.

There are two distinct processes for sending digital information:

- **Real-time keyboard-to-keyboard:** This is similar to texting from a smart device; simply type the message and hit "send." The software encodes the data to an audio signal, passes it through the computer radio interface, and then puts the radio in transmit mode. The signal is transmitted to the other radio. The received radio passes the signal to the recipient's computer through an interface, and the software decodes the data and displays it on the computer screen. MT63 and PSK31 are real-time keyboard-to-keyboard technologies.
- **Store-and-forward:** Email is a store-and-forward process. The message is typed into a software client before pressing send. The message then goes to a server or other device that holds the message for later retrieval by the recipient. Winlink is an example of store-and-forward technology. Automatic Packet Reporting System (APRS) radio can be used as both keyboard-to-keyboard and store-and-forward.

ANALOG VOICE VERSUS DIGITAL HAM RADIO

It's important for you to know the differences between analog and digital ham radio so that you can build a communication plan and setup that's best for your needs, environment, and budget. Analog voice will continue to be the default ham emergency communication (EMCOMM) mode for the foreseeable future, but digital data brings some useful and valuable assets to the party. Following is a pro and con list to help you decide if ham radio digital communication is good for your situation. Keep in mind that analog voice can convey the same information (except photos) as digital data technology, but digital data handles some information more effectively.

Analog Voice Pros:

- Simplicity: Push a button and talk.
- Human voice interaction: Hearing a person at the other end can be a comfort.
- Instant communication and feedback: No waiting for the message to go out and an answer to come back.
- Few failure points: Voice radio communication requires few electrical connections, which means there are fewer failure points than digital radio communication.

Analog Voice Cons:

- Limited data transfer: Reading and copying long lists or details can be tedious and difficult.
- Less robust signals: Susceptible to weak signals and interference.
- Requires more power: Voice transmissions use more bandwidth than digital, which equates to less distance at the same power.

Digital Data Pros:

- Error correction: Digital information is accurately received.
- Large data transmitted effectively: Long detailed lists and forms can be communicated when time isn't of the essence.
- Automation: Many modes can send and receive messages automatically or with minimal human interaction.

Digital Data Cons:

- Requires specialized equipment and software: More things to fail when it's most inconvenient.
- Requires additional power: Computers and smart devices add specific and additional power requirements.
- Difficult to deploy in the field: Outdoor and wilderness conditions are usually not conducive to enhanced electrical setups.

Winlink Global Radio Email

Winlink is one of the most powerful tools in radio communication because it allows you to send email communication over radio waves. Winlink provides email capability to places where the Internet isn't accessible. Its origins were in the sailing community, providing pleasure craft on the high seas with a way to share position reports, weather information, and other data via email. The Winlink system is a global network developed, built, and maintained by ham radio operators. It has grown and expanded into an important tool for emergency disaster radio communicators.

Emails are created, sent, and received with a proprietary email client with features similar to Outlook or Thunderbird. Email addresses use the standard Internet email format, and recipients do not need to be ham radio operators, nor do they need to have a ham radio license to send or reply to Winlink email addresses.

Winlink works by sending email messages that can include attachments by radio waves. After creating and addressing the email, the radio operator places the email in the "outbox." A radio attached to the computer is tuned to a frequency being monitored by a Winlink node that has Internet connectivity. Once the sending radio "connects" to the node, the radio transmits the email to the node, which relays it to and through the Internet to the recipient, who can read and reply just as they would with any email. If the recipient replies, the email is routed to the Winlink system, where it waits for the radio user to connect before sending it by radio wave.

Winlink emails are sent on open radio frequencies and are not secure or encrypted, so personal or private information should not be sent by Winlink.

Apps for Your Emergency Needs

Even though cellular and Internet service is often interrupted during large-scale disasters, it still makes sense to download a variety of apps that can be useful in the event Internet service is available. Many of these apps can also be used offline as well. While the cellular app landscape is constantly changing and evolving, following is a list of apps along with applicable uses to consider. These have been batched into several categories.

Weather and Disaster Information

- MyRadar Weather Radar
  - Download weather maps for offline viewing.
  - Provides basic weather updates and radar images even without active cellular service.
- NOAA Weather Radar
  - Allows downloading NOAA weather data and alerts for offline access.
  - Includes weather maps and radar imagery.
- Weather Underground
  - Provides hyper-local weather updates, including forecasts, radar maps, and severe weather alerts.
  - Features crowd-sourced data from personal weather stations to offer highly accurate, localized weather conditions.
  - Ideal for tracking storms, monitoring rainfall, and receiving real-time weather warnings.
- Hurricane Hound
  - Specifically designed to track hurricanes in real time.
  - Includes NOAA hurricane forecasts, projected paths, and severity updates.
  - Displays storm tracks on interactive maps to help users prepare for evacuation or sheltering.
  - Useful for residents in hurricane-prone areas during hurricane season.
- Natural Disaster Monitor
  - Monitors various natural disasters like earthquakes, tsunamis, floods, wildfires, and hurricanes.
  - Sends alerts about potential disasters in your area and allows tracking of events globally.
  - Provides early warnings to help you stay ahead of unfolding emergencies.
- Watch Duty: Wildfire Maps
  - Wildfire mapping and alert app powered by real people.
  - Get real-time updates about wildfires as well as evacuation orders and shelter information.

First Aid and Safety

- First Aid: American Red Cross
  - Offers advice for common medical emergencies including videos.
  - Allows you to customize weather alerts for your area.
- Pet First Aid
  - Focuses on providing first aid guidance for pets, including dogs and cats.
  - Offers step-by-step instructions for common emergencies like choking, poisoning, or injuries.
  - Includes a database for storing veterinary records and pet profiles.

Offline Maps and Navigation

- Maps.me
  - Offers fully offline maps with turn-by-turn navigation.
  - Download maps for specific regions in advance.
  - Features hiking trails and points of interest, making it useful for wilderness emergencies.
- Gaia GPS
  - Ideal for outdoor and wilderness navigation.
  - Provides detailed topographic maps that can be downloaded for offline use.
  - Includes route planning and GPS tracking, even without cellular service.
- Avenza Maps
  - Specialized for offline use with detailed maps, including US Forest Service maps and National Park Service maps.
  - Allows you to pin locations, measure distances, and navigate offline.
  - Excellent for wilderness and remote-area navigation.
- OsmAnd (OpenStreetMap Automated Navigation Directions)
  - Open-source mapping app that works entirely offline.
  - Provides road maps, hiking trails, and cycle routes.
  - Includes features like route planning and GPS tracking.

- onX Offroad
  - Turn-by-turn customizable route maps.
  - 3D maps.
  - Offline mode.
  - Points of interest and land ownership boundaries.
  - Route sharing with members of your group.

- Find my Phone—Family Locator
  - A GPS tracking app that helps locate family members or loved ones during an emergency.
  - Provides real-time location sharing and notifications for designated "safe zones."
  - Useful for coordinating with family members in crowded or chaotic situations.

Emergency Communication and Messaging

- Signal Private Messenger
  - Relies on Wi-Fi Direct for secure one-to-one and group messaging without Internet access.
  - Offers a simple interface with strong encryption, ensuring privacy and ease of use.
- Bridgefy
  - A Bluetooth-based messaging app for offline communication.
  - Ideal for coordinating with others within a short range (up to 330 feet).
- Briar
  - Designed for secure, offline communication via Bluetooth or Wi-Fi.
  - Works without centralized servers and is resistant to censorship or network shutdowns.
- White Mouse Private Messenger
  - Enables communication without Internet access among nearby devices (up to 100-meter radius), making it ideal for disaster scenarios.
  - Fortified with end-to-end encryption, no cloud storage, auto-deleting messages, and privacy-focused features like PIN-based connections and anti-screenshot measures.

- Supports text, photos, files, voice, and video sharing, along with voice and video calls, ensuring comprehensive communication options during emergencies.

- Zello Walkie-Talkie
  - Works offline for local communication using Wi-Fi or mesh networks.
  - Requires some initial setup to configure offline channels in advance.

Miscellaneous Disaster and Survival Apps

- Police Scanner Radio & Fire
  - A #1 police scanner that alerts you of breaking news.
  - Stay up-to-date with local news or listen to scanners from other areas.
  - Learn about traffic, emergencies, and public safety issues.

Quick Action Checklist

This chapter has discussed at length a variety of communication options, from using WiFi extenders and setting up localized mesh networks to using online and offline cellular apps. Even adding one or two of the digital tools in this chapter to your communication plan can boost flexibility and resilience.

Using the information provided in this chapter, now it's time to make some decisions about which of the digital tools and communication methods you want to add to the gear in your communication toolbox. Use the quick action checklist that follows to decide which of these make the most sense for you and your circumstances.

Using and Maximizing Cellular, Internet, and Wi-Fi Access in a Disaster

❏ Wi-Fi extenders

❏ Wi-Fi mesh networks

❏ Wide-area mesh networks

Cell Service but No Internet

❏ Email in emergencies

❏ Texting

Ham Radio Digital Communication

- ❏ Keyboard-to-keyboard communication (MT63, PSK31)
- ❏ Automatic Packet Reporting System (APRS)
- ❏ Winlink Global Radio Email

APRS Digital Communication

- ❏ GPS reporting

Apps to Consider Downloading

- ❏ MyRadar Weather Radar
- ❏ NOAA Weather Radar
- ❏ Weather Underground
- ❏ Hurricane Hound
- ❏ Natural Disaster Monitor
- ❏ Watch Duty: Wildfire Maps
- ❏ First Aid: American Red Cross
- ❏ Pet First Aid
- ❏ Maps.me
- ❏ Gaia GPS
- ❏ Avenza Maps
- ❏ OsmAnd (OpenStreetMap Automated Navigation Directions)
- ❏ onX Offroad
- ❏ Find my Phone—Family Locator
- ❏ Signal Private Messenger
- ❏ Bridgefy
- ❏ Briar
- ❏ White Mouse Private Messenger
- ❏ Zello Walkie-Talkie
- ❏ Police Scanner Radio & Fire

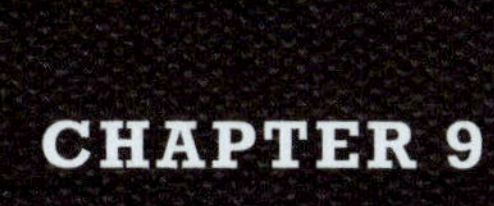

CHAPTER 9

SATELLITE COMMUNICATION TOOLS

In this chapter, you'll learn how satellite phones, messengers, and Internet services work and whether one of them makes sense to include in your emergency communication plan. These satellite communication tools are some of the most resilient communication options available when traditional infrastructure is wiped out. While many people think that satellite phones or messengers are only for extreme explorers on remote mountain peaks or jungle locations, more recent developments make these tools more affordable and practical than ever before. For family communication managers, they are absolutely worth exploring.

Your Lifeline to the Sky

Satellite phones, two-way satellite messengers, and Internet providers communicate with a network of satellites orbiting Earth. These satellites are not affected by disasters that might damage terrestrial cell towers. This means that they are not dependent on land-based infrastructure to operate. When it comes to communication during disasters that notoriously damage infrastructure, satellite technology becomes very interesting indeed.

Satellite phones have been useful communication tools during disasters all over the world dating back to the 1990s. As with all technology, dramatic improvements have increased while costs of owning and operating a satellite phone have decreased. This is now a tool that is more cost-efficient compared to previous years.

When it comes to satellite communications, there are satellite phones and there are two-way satellite messengers. Phones are what you'd expect, but messengers are limited to text messaging only. If your goal is to include some form of satellite-based communication tool within your gearbox, it's important that you have a clear understanding of what each category does and doesn't offer.

Satellite Phones

Choosing a satellite phone is a delicate balance of service, features, cost, and goals. This section will help you weigh those factors to determine if one is right for you. While there are several options for satellite phones these days, following are four of the top options to consider. A convenient list of pros and cons should help you decide which model (if any) is right for you.

At the time of this writing, many of these satellite phone models can be acquired for free with a twenty-four-month service contract from sites like www.bluecosmo.com. These contracts vary in price depending on the number of minutes needed each month, but they start at $54 per month. Without the service contract, you can expect to pay $800 and up for the device itself. Just the phone alone can be purchased from several retailers online and will be shipped with a SIM card for activating it upon arrival. Once you own the phone, you can choose a monthly airtime plan or buy prepaid minutes.

IRIDIUM GO!

This is a portable satellite Wi-Fi hot spot that lets you make voice calls, send messages, and access email using your smartphone.

Pros:

- Offers voice calling, SMS (with high character limit), and email capabilities.
- Includes GPS tracking and a programmable one-touch SOS button.
- Functions as a mobile hot spot for up to five devices.
- Compact with a stowable antenna.

Cons:

- Requires a smartphone for full functionality and voice calls.
- Connection can be inconsistent, preventing effective communication.
- Limited battery life compared to other models.
- Heavy and bulky compared to other satellite communication devices.

INMARSAT ISATPHONE 2

This is a rugged and affordable satellite phone designed for reliable voice communication in remote areas around the world. (www.inmarsat.com; www.bluecosmo.com)

Satellite phone being used in a remote location without cellular service.

Pros:

- Excellent value for the price, with a variety of affordable service plans.
- Long battery life: 8 hours talk time and 160 hours standby.
- Integrated SOS button connects to the GEOS emergency rescue center.
- Durable, weather-resistant design with a large, easy-to-use interface.

Cons:

- Coverage excludes polar regions.
- Directional antenna requires precise alignment for reliable connectivity.
- Sound quality and slight delay can be bothersome in some conditions.

IRIDIUM 9555

This is a compact, reliable satellite phone with truly global coverage. It is a trusted choice for remote communication. (www.iridium.com/products/iridium-9555/)

Pros:

- Extensive global coverage, including polar regions.
- Crystal-clear voice quality in most conditions.
- Programmable SOS button for emergency response.
- Affordable monthly plans with free incoming calls and texts.

Cons:

- Short battery life (4 hours talk time); requires additional batteries.
- Not waterproof or IP-rated for harsh conditions.
- Does not include built-in GPS capabilities.

GLOBALSTAR GSP-1700

This is a lightweight, entry-level satellite phone ideal for customers primarily needing coverage in North America. Although new units are no longer in production, refurbished units are still available. (www.globalstar.com)

Price: $400-plus (phone is no longer in production; this price is for old stock or refurbished)

Pros:

- Budget-friendly option with US-based phone numbers at no extra cost.
- Compact and lightweight design.
- Fast data speeds for texts and coordinates.
- Good voice quality for North America coverage.

Cons:

- Limited coverage outside North America; numerous dead zones.
- Phone is no longer in production, but service plans are still available.
- Shorter battery life compared to other models.

DOES A SATELLITE PHONE MAKE SENSE FOR THE AVERAGE PERSON?

Before you invest in a satellite phone, you should determine if this purchase makes sense for your lifestyle, goals, and budget. While many people love the connectivity that satellite phones bring to the communications lineup, they can be expensive in both device cost and monthly plans. These are tools used primarily by off-grid adventurers, hunters, travelers, expeditions, and remote industries. If you have a job or lifestyle that brings you out of cellular service frequently and you're also wanting a device that can offer coverage during disaster when traditional forms of communication are disrupted, then a satellite phone makes a lot of sense. But if it is just for disaster preparedness, then the up-front and monthly expenditure might not be worth it. One of the radio types discussed in previous chapters likely makes the most sense for the common person seeking off-grid communication tools.

It is worth noting, however, that there are providers that rent satellite phones for as low as $29.99 per week (at the time of this writing). If you live in areas that are predictably prone to disasters during certain seasons, such as hurricanes, renting a satellite phone for a "disaster season" is an option without the long-term commitment. Renting can also allow you to test-drive satellite phone technology for a fraction of the cost to help make a more educated decision. An online search for "satellite phone rental" will provide numerous options.

OPERATING A SATELLITE PHONE

For the most part, operating a satellite phone is very similar to operating a regular cell phone and will be intuitive to those who already use cell phones. The exceptions are the models, such as the Iridium GO!, which must be paired with a smartphone in order to have full functionality and voice calls.

While satellite phones have many similarities to regular cell phones, there are a few operational differences and limitations one can expect. These include:

- **Line of sight:** Satellite phones must have a direct line of sight between the phone and the satellite. Being inside of a building, cave, or even forest will dramatically affect reception.
- **Signal delay:** Compared to cell phones, you can expect a slight delay when communicating with satellite technology.
- **Data speed:** In addition to a signal delay, data speed is often much slower than what you experience with your cell phones on ground level. Some models of satellite phones lack Internet access altogether.
- **Battery life:** The battery life of satellite phones is typically much shorter than modern smartphones. The battery drains even faster while in remote areas with a weak signal.

Two-Way Satellite Communicators

If you don't need voice messages but like the idea and functionality of satellite communication, then a two-way communicator might be the best choice. Two-way satellite communicators and satellite texting devices are a cost-effective alternative to full-fledged satellite phones and Internet services, such as Starlink (detailed next). These devices aren't capable of voice communication, but you can share texts and GPS coordinates with colleagues and family members when in areas without cell service. As with any satellite device, they work best with a clear, unobstructed view of the sky, and texts can take several minutes to be sent even in optimal conditions. These satellite texting devices, with their ability to alert first responders with an SOS feature, bring peace of mind to thousands of backcountry adventurers each year.

These communicators are interesting because they actually use two types of satellite technology. First, they send and receive the messages using a satellite communication network. Most of them use one of the satellite networks from the previously mentioned satellite phones. However, the emergency location information is established by utilizing GPS. The device communicates with satellites orbiting Earth to determine your exact location and then sends that information utilizing a different network of satellites. An added bonus is that some models offer GPS satellite navigation and can even pair with a smartphone. These features have applications that can apply to disaster evacuation or even navigating within a disaster area without cellular service or paper maps.

To sum up the key features of two-way satellite communicators, here is what you can expect:

- Two-way text-based messaging (can take several minutes for delivery; note some models/brands only offer the ability to send messages)
- GPS location tracking
- SOS feature to send GPS coordinates to rescue personnel
- Navigation (some models)
- Less expensive than satellite phones

If a two-way satellite communicator sounds like a tool you'd be interested in, following is a short list of the most popular. All of the two-way satellite communicators listed include an SOS feature that contacts the appropriate first responders with your GPS coordinates and position check-ins. They all also require a monthly subscription for full service.

GARMIN INREACH

Garmin is the leader in GPS and satellite communication devices. They offer models ranging from simple communication (texting and SOS) devices to full-feature navigation tools with optional inReach capability. Garmin uses the Iridium satellite network.

Website: www.garmin.com/en-US/c/outdoor-recreation/satellite-communicators

Price: $249 and up

Pros:

- Leader in the GPS industry.
- Excellent battery life.
- Wide selection of products, features, and options.
- Extensive SOS response network.
- Uses satellite, cellular, and Wi-Fi technology.
- Optional weather, voice, and photo messages.

SPOT X and Garmin inReach satellite texting devices. Both come with tethers to attach the device to a backpack to maintain line of sight with satellites. Some users prefer the inReach's compact size, while others prefer a larger footprint with a full QWERTY keyboard. Both feature SOS alerting.

Cons:

- Expensive initial cost.
- The user interface can be confusing.
- No dedicated phone number.

SPOT X

The SPOT X is SPOT's flagship device. It's a stand-alone satellite texting device that doesn't require tethering to a smart device. The SPOT Gen4 has a more attractive price point than the SPOT X but requires tethering to a smart device for full functionality. SPOT uses the Globalstar satellite network, which is more regional than Iridium's global coverage. Coverage is excellent in the Americas and most of Europe but can be spotty in other continents.

Website: www.findmespot.com

Price: SPOT X: $249; Gen4: $149

Pros:

- No tethering is required (SPOT X).
- QWERTY keyboard (SPOT X).
- Attractive price point.
- Affordable subscriptions.
- Dedicated phone number.

Cons:

- Minimal navigation features.
- Larger than comparable devices.
- No cellular or Wi-Fi connectivity.

ZOLEO

ZOLEO has a no-nonsense approach to satellite texting. It requires tethering to a phone for full functionality, but the app provides a familiar texting experience. Like Garmin, ZOLEO uses the Iridium satellite network for global coverage.

Website: www.zoleo.com

Price: $199 (plus subscription)

Pros:

- Easy to use.
- Uses satellite, cellular, and Wi-Fi.
- Includes weather info and ZOLEO Medical Assist feature for nonemergency advice as part of the standard service.

Cons:

- Limited functionality.
- Messaging is dependent on pairing with a phone or tablet app.
- Lacks stand-alone voice calling capabilities.

APPLE IPHONE SATELLITE MESSAGING

Apple's entry into the satellite messaging world with the iPhone 14 may be a game changer, but the jury is still out. If you already own an iPhone 14 or are already planning to upgrade, this may be the best option for you. However, iPhone satellite messaging uses the Globalstar network like the previously mentioned SPOT X. Also, this puts all of your eggs in one basket. If your phone is damaged or the battery dies, you'll also lose satellite messaging.

Website: https://support.apple.com/en-us/120930

Price: $699 and up (if you don't already own an iPhone 14)

Pros:

- Seamless integration with your iPhone.
- No learning curve.

Cons:

- Not all Globalstar areas are approved for use by Apple.
- All-in-one device.

At the time of this writing, other smartphone manufacturers are introducing satellite SOS features with full texting to follow soon after.

GPS Coordinates for Search and Rescue

There are two methods to establish geolocations around the globe: latitude/longitude (Lat-Long) and the United States National Grid/Military Grid Reference System (USNG/MGRS). Most people are familiar with Lat-Lon, but the grid reference system is a more effective, less complicated, and precise way to identify a location when street address information isn't available, such as in the wilderness or on open water.

We recommend using the USNG/MGRS system because it's so easy to use. Also, search and rescue teams, state divisions of emergency management, and FEMA have standardized on it. Most GPS units can be set up to use USNG/MGRS.

LATITUDE/LONGITUDE

Latitude and longitude (Lat-Long) coordinates establish specific locations using angular measurements. The measurements are expressed in three forms: decimal degrees, decimal minutes, and degrees, minutes, seconds. Lat-Long has been used for centuries and is the "native language" of GPS. However, it has significant downsides for use in an emergency. The two most significant cons of Lat-Long are its complexity and distortion when plotting spherical locations on a flat map.

Pros:

- Widespread use.
- Familiar concept.

Cons:

- Requires specialized knowledge.
- Distances and direction are distorted when translating from globe to map.
- Multiple formats create confusion.

GRID REFERENCE

There are two primary grid reference systems: the United States National Grid (USNG) and the Military Grid Reference System (MGRS). The USNG is based on the MGRS, so they can be thought of as the same thing. The main difference is that USNG coordinates are written with spaces, so they're easier to read.

The USNG/MGRS system divides the globe into a grid of 100,000-meter squares, which can be subdivided further down to as small as 1 square meter. It accomplishes this by adding more digits to the coordinates.

For example, "17R MP 15 37" is the USNG coordinates for a 1,000-square-meter area in Jennings State Forest in Florida. The "17R MP" indicates the top-level 100,000-meter square. The "15 37" indicates the 1,000-square-meter area in Jennings State Forest. The precision can be refined to 100 square meters by adding one digit to the 15 and 37, each. "157 372" (The precision at this point makes the 17R MP irrelevant, so it can be dropped.)

You can refine the location all the way down to 1 square meter at ten digits: "15772 37253," but a 10-square-meter area, with eight digits, is specific enough to locate a lost hiker or injured hunter.

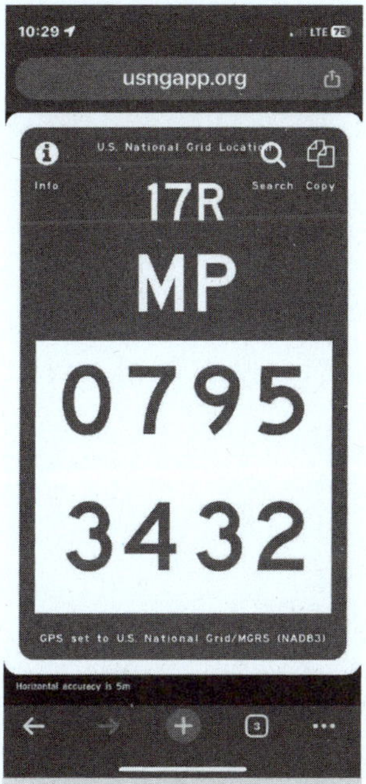

A screenshot of USNG coordinates displayed in the usngapp.org browser-based app. A screenshot like this could be texted to a relative or friend to provide first responders with their location in an emergency. The eight digits "0795 3432" define the location within 1 square meter.

Pros:

- Easy to understand.
- Standardized by search and rescue, FEMA, etc.
- Accurate direction and distance.
- Enhanced precision.

Cons:

- Possible distortion at grid edges.
- Less familiar.

The browser-based app at usngapp.org is the easiest way to find your USNG coordinates. Try bookmarking it in your favorite smartphone browser for quick access. If faced with a search-and-rescue situation, bring up the app, take a screenshot, and text it to an emergency contact. They can give the USNG coordinates to any first responder dispatcher to send help. By the way, the usngapp.org app, and similar apps like MyUSNG, FindMeSAR, and USNG Me, have offline functionality.

WHAT3WORDS

While not used often by emergency services, this is a system that could help you communicate your location to family and friends. What3words is a relatively new grid-based location system that aims to simplify coordinates into common words. The concept is to identify any 3-meter square on the planet by three specific, but unrelated words. What3words has proven to be a handy tool for meeting up with friends, but the jury is still out on its effectiveness in search and rescue.

Pros:

- Easy to use.
- Short "coordinates."
- Offline functionality.

Cons:

- Not officially adopted by search and rescue or first responders.
- Controlled by a private business.

Satellite Internet

In the scope of disaster communication, satellite technology is no longer limited to stand-alone satellite phones or two-way satellite communicators. In recent years, this technology is now being used to provide satellite-based Internet service. If staying online is a part of your communications strategy, this section will help you decide which satellite Internet service may be a best fit for your custom plan. The three leading satellite Internet providers are Starlink, Hughesnet, and Viasat.

As you'll see in the following information, Starlink has the fastest Internet speeds. This is because Starlink uses a constellation of thousands of low Earth orbit (LEO) satellites about 350 miles high. Hughesnet and Viasat use three and four geostationary satellites, respectively, in high Earth orbit (HEO), about 22,000 miles high. The increased distance accounts for the increased latency.

Also, Starlink's network of satellites is much more resilient than Hughesnet's or Viasat's three or four. If Hughesnet or Viasat were to lose just one satellite because of a solar storm or malfunction, their capacity would be reduced by 25–33 percent.

HUGHESNET

Hughesnet was the first satellite Internet provider. It offers high-speed Internet access to areas without wired Internet providers.

- Download/Upload speeds: 100 Mbps/5 Mbps
- Latency: 600–700 ms
- Subscription: Starting at $49
- Equipment: Starting at $299
- Setup: Professional installation required
- Complex setup makes portability impractical

VIASAT

Viasat provides satellite Internet service to rural, remote, and hard-to-reach areas with technology similar to Hughesnet.

- Download/Upload speeds: 150 Mbps/6 Mbps
- Latency: 500–800 ms
- Subscription: Starting at $99
- Equipment: Starting at $250 (leasing is available)
- Setup: Professional setup required
- Complex setup makes portability impractical

STARLINK

Starlink is the most expensive option, but prices are dropping rapidly, and there is a variety of flexible pricing options. Starlink's resilience, small footprint, incorporated Wi-Fi router, and easy setup make it a good recommendation for any family wishing to add satellite Internet to their emergency communication plan.

Starlink is opening new possibilities for disaster emergency communication. Disaster relief organizations like The Salvation Army and the Red Cross have used Starlink technology in several recent disasters, such as Hurricane Milton in 2024 and the LA wildfires in 2025. In some instances, Starlink is replacing radio HF technology for long-distance communication during disaster recovery efforts.

Starlink is available for personal use and can provide Internet connectivity for up to 128–254 simultaneous connections. However, performance is degraded with increased traffic. In today's day and age, Internet connectivity has countless benefits to a family communication manager. What's even more attractive is that Starlink doesn't have to be purchased as a "backup" Internet provider. It can be used as the main provider during normal times as well. This makes the economics of this option even more sensible. As long as backup power is established through one of the options in Chapter 3, Starlink can provide Internet service during a crisis

A Starlink Mini powered by a lithium-iron phosphate battery charged by a solar panel.

The portable Starlink Mini fits in a backpack, takes up little room on a picnic table, and even works while resting on your dashboard as you drive down the road. Paired with a roaming subscription package, the Mini is worth considering for both bug in and bug out scenarios.

- Download/Upload speeds: 220 Mbps/20 Mbps
- Latency: 33–48 ms
- Subscription: Starting at $80
- Equipment: Starting at $349
- Setup: Do it yourself in minutes
- Portable

Using Starlink for Group and Community Emergency Communications

One incredible real-life application for Starlink satellite technology is to help set up a group or neighborhood communication hub post-disaster. This applies to not only communication responders who deploy into disaster zones but also for the average person who wishes to help set up communications for friends, neighbors, and family who live in close proximity.

Pairing Starlink with mesh Wi-Fi can allow Internet service to reach multiple households in the neighborhood. This can open lines of communication for many people at the same time and can take the pressure off of radio use if there aren't very many devices to share.

This technology is an excellent addition to not only personal and neighborhood readiness kits, but also to organizations, churches, businesses, community disaster squads, and schools. The ability to send mass emails to parents, employees, or members is a communication luxury during disasters and can help to achieve multiple goals. It can be used with apps like Zello or Signal for group texting over Wi-Fi, which adds even more depth to a communication plan.

Starlink Internet and two-way radios combine to make a very powerful communication system. The radios can be used for local voice messaging and Starlink can be used for distant text and email. These two options solve many communication problems—all entirely off-grid except for power.

The Future of Satellite

As exciting as satellite technology is currently, the best is yet to come. While we certainly can't predict the future, history tells us that this technology will not only get smaller in size but also much more affordable to use. As mentioned, Apple has already expanded into satellite technology as of the iPhone 14 and other cell phone manufacturers are in various stages of developing similar offerings. These adaptations literally put satellite technology in our pockets.

The Starlink Mini combined with a Starlink Roam Internet service plan is already an amazing offering for portable off-grid Wi-Fi service in a very small package. There is no doubt this package will get even smaller, more affordable, and even more powerful. The horizon is not only filled with satellites but also a bright future for those who seek connectivity during tumultuous times.

Satellite Communication Vulnerabilities

Individual satellite devices are susceptible to outages caused by weather, tree canopies, mountains, and so on. Satellite signal lock can take up to 30 minutes and text throughput can take 15 minutes or more to be sent if the signal is degraded by obstructions. These vulnerabilities are usually short-term inconveniences.

Human error can render satellite communication inert for thousands, even millions, of people over multiple continents. One such event was a Starlink outage in 2024, which affected more than 40,000 Starlink users on three continents and lasted 45 minutes. Starlink reported that it was caused by an unexpected certificate expiration. But it's not beyond imagination that a cyberattack directed at satellite providers could produce similar results, but with wider-spread and longer-lasting disruption.

Of course, a massive solar storm—similar to the 1859 Carrington Event—could wipe out entire constellations of communication satellites. Satellite phones, GPS units, and satellite texting devices would all be useless. It would take years to fully recover global satellite coverage. The good news is that Starlink reports less than 30 percent of its users experience an outage over any ninety-day period. Also, even though Earth experiences solar events several times a year, storms like the Carrington Event are extremely rare.

Quick Action Checklist

It's time to decide which type of satellite communication you want to add to your communication toolbox. Use the information in this chapter to determine what makes the most sense for your circumstances. Consider these points:

- Is the terrain around your location conducive to line of sight to satellites?
- Does your situation justify the cost of satellite voice communication, or would a satellite texting device suffice?
- Which is more reliable for your situation, a stand-alone satellite communication device or one that requires a smart device?
- If you're using a GPS device, have you set it to use a grid system?
- Have you downloaded or accessed a USNG app?
- Does your situation require off-grid high bandwidth Internet access such as Starlink?

PART 4

YOUR COMMUNICATION PLAN

So far this book has discussed radio services, types of radios, and also the tools and technologies of digital and satellite communication. At this stage, you have made decisions about backup power, which radio services make the most sense for you, which radio setups to acquire, and which licenses are necessary to operate those radios. Your emergency communication strategy is coming together, but you may still feel like things are a bit disorganized. You're now at the part of the process where you bring all of these decisions together in a very logical and turnkey format.

Emergencies are unpredictable and chaotic, and a well-structured communication plan ensures a system of good, solid decisions are made in the midst of the storm. It minimizes confusion, reduces panic, and gives each person in your party roles, responsibilities, and step-by-step actions to take. Whether it's regrouping at predetermined meeting points, practicing drills, or maintaining devices, this part provides practical advice for helping you create a communication strategy tailored to your family's or group's needs.

Let's now put theory into practice. As you transition from learning to doing, it's time to roll up your sleeves and put the final pieces of the emergency communication puzzle into place. All the decisions you've made thus far will now be formulated into your official Family Communication Plan.

HOW TO CREATE A COMMUNICATION PLAN

From backup power and radio service preferences to radio setups and receivers, you've likely identified many tools and resources that meet your specific communication goals, whether those be for yourself, family, or neighborhood. Now it is time to build the plan into which these tools will fit. Communication tools are only useful when combined with an effective and efficient plan. In this chapter, you will create a customized Family Communication Plan as well as a Communications Power Plan.

The Power of a Plan

Your customized Family Communication Plan will outline the directives and information for two main aspects of communication if the communication grid is compromised. These include:

1. Plans for locating and communicating with family members and/or local team members.
2. Plans for communicating with contacts outside of the disaster zone.

And, because electricity to power your communication tools is so important, you will also complete an outline of your Communications Power Plan to make sure those plans are in place as well. (You'll be pulling some of the decisions you made back in Chapter 3 to complete this section.)

With plans in place for these particular components, you are ready to not only locate and gather family members who may be in different locations in a regional disaster zone, but also communicate outside of the disaster zone to secure help, resources, or make plans for evacuation.

Pre-Disaster Communications Prep

It's important to note that any plan, including your communication plan, is most effective when everyone understands it and has practiced it beforehand. The time to review and execute the plan for the first time is not when a disaster strikes. It is critical to review all emergency communication plans in advance of an event happening. There is nothing more effective than practice to calm nerves in the midst of a crisis.

FAMILY/GROUP MEETING

It's important when this plan is completed that you hold an official group or Family Communication Plan meeting. The idea of a formal meeting helps to frame the information in the light it deserves. This is the opportunity to go over all the items you'll be documenting in this chapter, including communication roles, printed materials, meeting points, and even the location of communication plan documents, tools, and supplies.

ENCOURAGE PARTICIPATION

An emergency communication plan is as boring as the presenter. It's important to make this an exciting moment for all attendees. Here are a few easy and fun ways to do this:

- This is an excellent opportunity to distribute radios for those who will be using their own handheld. Even if younger members aren't licensed for ham, consider picking up some inexpensive FRS walkie-talkies to make sure everyone is included.
- Have fun with brainstorming radio call signs if using FRS or CB radios. This is especially fun for younger communicators.

- Run a mock communication drill! Use one of the drills detailed in Chapter 11 or design your own. There's nothing more fun than using new gear in a radio game of cat and mouse.
- Inevitably, there will be some items within the plan that need to be completed during the meeting. This keeps the meeting active. Have pens or pencils on hand so that each member can complete missing data for members that may not be living in the same household.
- Open the floor for Q&A. Instead of just presenting information, design the meeting to be a conversation that encourages questions about topics such as plan activation triggers and potential disaster scenarios.

PLAN DISTRIBUTION

Plan to have physical copies of the full emergency communication plan for each member to complete and take home with them. To make digital distribution of the communication plan that you'll create in this chapter easier, consider creating QR codes for team members to scan with their devices to quickly and immediately download the digital versions on their cell phones and/or tablets once you've updated the plans with information gathered from everyone at the meeting.

SETTING EXPECTATIONS

Managing expectations is a good character trait for any leader. This first meeting is the best time to set expectations for communication team members. Each team leader's expectations will be different. This portion of the meeting doesn't have to have an overly rigid tone, but it should be regarded as important. Here are some questions to consider:

- Are all team members expected to learn radio communications? If so, which services and setups?
- Are all team members required to choose a communication role (described in the next section)?
- Are all team members required to participate in routine drills?
- Who is responsible for activating the communication plan, and how?

But before breaking down all the items that should be included in a Family Communication Plan, it's important to broach the topic of communication roles.

Communication Roles

Virtually every formal communication team—whether that team works in the professional disaster readiness space or in a military setting—has clearly defined communication roles. Clearly defined roles not only help when training (see Chapter 11) but also have numerous benefits to a family or team. Some of these include:

- Reducing confusion.
- Preventing redundancy and double work.
- Promoting accountability and personal responsibility.
- Encouraging inclusion, involvement, and a sense of importance for all family or team members.
- Adding a layer of realism to practice drills.

While defining communication roles is certainly optional, it is an aspect of emergency communication that can help make a well-defined plan even more effective. Here are some suggested communication roles and descriptions that can be assigned to members of your own family or team.

- **Lead communicator:** This person is essentially the person in charge of communication decisions and is responsible for activating the family or group communication plan. The person in this role is likely the most practiced and experienced with equipment and is the one primarily responsible for sending messages in an emergency.
- **Log keeper:** This person is in charge of recording and keeping track of information gained from all communication methods. This not only includes the location of all members of the family or team but also emergency updates, information, and messages from others that relate to the scenario.
- **Check-in coordinator:** For families or teams with scheduled check-in times, this person makes sure all the core team members are sending/

receiving messages at these predetermined times. They also keep track of who else has checked in or missed a check-in.

- **Secondary communicator:** This person takes charge of communications in the event the lead communicator is unavailable, missing, preoccupied, or injured. This person should be versed and practiced with all communication tools and procedures.
- **Runner:** A runner is responsible for hand delivering messages to nearby neighbors or contacts should they not be equipped with backup communication tools.
- **Power lead:** This person is responsible for setting up and maintaining the batteries and equipment needed to power the communication tools. Responsibilities can include charging batteries, fueling generators, and setting up solar arrays.
- **Junior communicator:** Assigning junior communicator roles to younger team members is a great way to engage children and to help them feel a part of the team. They can get their own call sign and help other communicators with things like packing, listening to incoming messages, or charging batteries.

To build a more adaptable and robust communications team, consider rotating roles every few months. This helps other team members to learn other aspects of the plan, which in turn builds confidence and ability. It also prepares the team for things that can happen in real-life events, such as injuries.

With these roles in consideration, it's now time to put pen to paper and officially start recording the details of your plan. It is recommended that hard copies of the following documents be kept in all households involved with your communication plan. Each member included in your plan should not only be familiar with each aspect but also have scanned copies on their phones and even printed versions in their purses, backpacks, and vehicles. Following is a breakdown with descriptions of all information that should be included in your communication plan. Printer-friendly form versions of the plans can be acquired for free by visiting www.creekstewart.com/emergencycommunications101. These can be printed, filled out, added to a three-ring binder, and distributed accordingly.

Family Communication Plan: Local Communications

Following are each of the main components that need to be included for local communications. This is communication between family members, team members, and even neighbors.

- **Emergency contacts:** A full list of emergency contacts. This list includes all family members, local fire station, police, and any other contacts included in your communication circle. Each contact should list full name, cell phone number, email, home address, social media accounts, communication role title, and any applicable radio channels or frequencies.
- **ICE numbers:** Make sure that In Case of Emergency (ICE) numbers are entered into every family member's phone. These are emergency contact numbers that can be accessed by first responders just in case you are unconscious or injured. Enter the contact name as ICE-1-NAME. For example, your wife might be entered as ICE-1-WIFE or your husband might be entered as ICE-1-HUSBAND.
- **Emergency meeting places:** It is very possible that family members could be spread across a city or region in the event of a sudden and unexpected disaster scenario. If this happens, you need to have three predetermined unique emergency meeting places established. Each of these locations and addresses should be listed on your Family Communication Plan paperwork. Where applicable, also include emails, phone numbers, and social media account information. Be sure to include a physical copy of directions to the out-of-town location, such as an atlas, detailing multiple routes. There are spaces for this information in the downloadable forms at www.creekstewart.com/emergencycommunications101. The three meeting places are as follows:
  - **Immediate location:** Somewhere a safe distance from your home but still in the immediate area just in case there's a fire or something similar. This meeting place allows everyone to be quickly accounted for. Examples are a swing set, a certain tree, or the mailbox.

- **Primary in-town location:** An in-town family meeting place just in case your home is inaccessible. Examples include a favorite park, a church, or a unique landmark.
- **Primary out-of-town location:** An out-of-town meeting place in the event your home and in-town meeting place are both inaccessible. Examples might include a campground, a friend's house, or a relative's house. The distance of the contact should be 1–2 hours away.

- **Parent/Guardian workplace information:** This information should include address, emergency contact information, and any relevant evacuation and/or emergency disaster plans that exist. If updates during disasters are sent via text message or posted on social media channels, be sure to also know how to access these.
- **Child school and/or daycare information:** This information should include address, emergency contact information, and any relevant evacuation and/or emergency disaster plans that exist. If updates during disasters are sent via text message or posted on social media channels, be sure to also know how to access these.
- **Detailed family information:** Included in this section should be the following items for each family member:
  - Name
  - Date of birth
  - Social Security number
  - Medical conditions
  - Prescription medicines
- **Medical contacts:** This section should include name, address, email, and emergency contact phone numbers for all applicable medical professionals related to your family's health. These may include family doctor, pediatrician, specialist doctor, dentist, or therapist.
- **Insurance information:** It is also a good idea to have all insurance account numbers, contacts, phone numbers, and emails. This includes health, home, property, and vehicle.
- **Alternate communication details:** If traditional modes of communication such as cell phones, landlines, and Internet aren't working, it is critical that each family member know the following:

- **Communication kit location:** Alternate communication radios, batteries, and chargers should be kept together in a consistent location.
- **Rally channels/frequencies:** Your family should choose "rally" channels or frequencies to tune into during an emergency. For ham or GMRS radios, this will probably be a repeater frequency if one is available. If a repeater is not available or for FRS radios, it will be a simplex, or radio-to-radio, channel. Consider recording the following:
  - **Primary repeater frequency/channel information:** Your family should choose a primary ham radio repeater frequency, GMRS channel, or FRS channel so that everyone knows where to tune into if they are separated.
  - **Second backup repeater frequency/channel information:** Your family should choose a second backup ham radio repeater frequency, GMRS channel, or FRS channel so that everyone knows where to tune into if they are separated.
  - **Third backup repeater frequency/channel information:** Your family should choose a third backup ham radio repeater frequency, GMRS channel, or FRS channel so that everyone knows where to tune into if they are separated.
  - **Fourth backup simplex frequency/channel information:** Your family should choose a fourth backup ham radio simplex frequency, GMRS channel, or FRS channel so that everyone knows where to tune into if they are separated.
  - **Fifth backup simplex frequency/channel information:** Your family should choose a fifth backup ham radio simplex frequency, GMRS channel, or FRS channel so that everyone knows where to tune into if they are separated.
- **Established monitoring time:** For efficiency and routine check-ins, a specific time should be chosen to monitor and/or check in on the previously listed frequencies/channels. Whether this is on the 30-minute mark of every hour or the first and last 15 minutes of every hour, choose two specific times per hour for checking in and monitoring for messages from family and local contacts.

Family Communication Plan: Out-of-Town Communications

In addition to the previous information, a detailed section for out-of-town communications should be included. Most resources only recommend one out-of-town contact, however, it is wise to establish three in case the disaster is extremely large and prevents you from reaching or traveling to your primary out-of-town contact. You have already identified one of these out-of-town contacts as the primary in the previous section that is 1–2 hours away. Now choose two more according to the following descriptions:

- **Second out-of-town contact: 3–5 hours away:** This distance provides you with more evacuation flexibility if there are road closures, road damage, or if the disaster covers a larger area than planned for with your primary out-of-town contact. Circumstances could also prevent you from getting in touch with your primary contact and confirming they are available to receive you and your family.
- **Third out-of-town contact: 1–3 states away:** Should the scope of the disaster require farther evacuation, or if your previous two contacts are unavailable or also affected, having a third out-of-town contact 1–3 states away is a smart decision that takes very little effort and has a lot of upsides. This is especially important if you live in an area prone to wide sweeping natural disasters such as hurricanes.

The following information for each of these contacts should be included with your paperwork:

- Emergency contact name
- Phone number
- Email
- Social media accounts
- Address
- Primary predetermined ham radio frequency (if applicable)
- Secondary predetermined ham radio frequency (if applicable)

- Predetermined GMRS radio channel (if applicable)
- Secondary GMRS radio channel (if applicable)
- Physical copies of directions (such as an atlas) detailing multiple routes

Neighborhood Communication Plan

While the previous information for local and out-of-town communications revolves around a Family Communication Plan, this documentation can be quickly and easily adapted to create a Neighborhood Communication Plan (or a plan for any other group) as well. In fact, the same forms can be used but it's likely that not all the data will be necessary for a Neighborhood Communication Plan.

History tells us that our neighbors are our first responders in a crisis and vice versa. A next natural step after creating a family plan is to expand the communication net to homes in your neighborhood or apartment complex (when applicable).

Benefits of a Neighborhood Communication Plan include:

- Faster access to help, especially for the more vulnerable neighbors who may be elderly or have children.
- Sharing information in real time via the comfort of your home instead of walking around the neighborhood.
- Emotional reassurance for those who might be less prepared to deal with a crisis.
- Potential resource sharing (food, fuel, medical supplies, power tools, and so on).

Importance of Discreet Communications

Discretion in communications was mentioned in Chapter 7, but it is worth repeating here as you assemble the physical documents of your communication plan. It's important to consider discretion with messaging too. This is especially true with radio communications such as ham, GMRS, FRS, CB, and MURS where other people might be listening in on your conversations.

If you remember from Chapter 7, secret codes, hidden meanings, and encryption are illegal on all personal radio services. However, discretion is wise. Much of this discretionary language can be included in the Family Communication Plan. Tactical call signs, also discussed in Chapter 7, can be helpful in maintaining "on-air" discretion.

Consider these messages:

- "This is Hamilton 1. We're headed to the primary in-town location. Please confirm. Over."
- "This is Hamilton 2. Too much interference. Switching to third backup frequency. Please confirm. Over."

The "primary in-town location" and "third backup frequency" simply match the headings for those entries on the Family Communication Plan. Using this language helps all people with a copy of the plan know exactly what you're communicating.

These messages deliver a very specific directive to members of the team who have access to the communication plan, but very vague information to anyone else who may be listening. In neither instance is sensitive information revealed. Communication language can be as simple or complex as you want, but for most Family Communication Plans, simple and easy is best. Be sure to review pro words, Q Codes and 10 Codes in Chapter 6 for more ideas. Consider the following guidelines when incorporating code into your communication dialogue:

- Make sure any coding or code names are clearly documented on your Family Communication Plan documents.
- Always avoid using real names.
- Always avoid using location markers or specific addresses.
- Include using all language in lifestyle integration and routine drills to build habits and familiarity.

With all important information recorded for communication roles, local communications, and out-of-town communications, now it's time to document the section for your Communications Power Plan.

Communications Power Plan

Using the forms from www.creekstewart.com/emergencycommunications101 or on a separate document, it's important to make final decisions and document your plan for how you'll be powering the communication tools that you've decided to purchase from the previous chapters. Now, it's time to combine those decisions with the ones made in Chapter 3 and put details on paper as to exactly what power solutions will be in place for the communication tools that will be used in your plan.

Your Communications Power Plan should be organized by tiers so that you or someone else in your party can quickly reference it based upon what actions your party is taking during a disaster such as sheltering in place or evacuation. Again, the purpose of this is to make as many decisions as possible in advance so that this information is turnkey in the time of crisis.

If you're creating your own documents using blank paper or other computer software rather than downloading the forms from www.creekstewart.com/emergencycommunications101, you'll need to create a heading for each of the following tiers:

- **Tier 1:** Personal Power
  - Primary uses will be for short-term power outages, bug out evacuations, and mobile communications.
- **Tier 2:** Device Power Support
  - Primary uses will be for short-term power outages, bug out evacuations, mobile communications, or support once a destination is reached.
- **Tier 3:** Household Power Support
  - Primary uses will be for multiday power outages during a shelter-in-place scenario or to set up a temporary base camp during an evacuation either for personal or professional use.
- **Tier 4:** Whole-House Automatic Backup Power
  - Primary use is for a long-term power outage during a shelter-in-place scenario.

Each of these tiers should include the following information for each communication tool that requires power:

- Device to power
- Primary power source
- Backup method
- All power accessories needed
- Documentation, such as manuals or user guides
- Storage location
- Maintenance schedule
- Lead Communicator for this tier

Activation Triggers

In addition to having a clear and documented step-by-step communications and power plan, it's also important that each family or team member understands exactly when the plan should be activated. Knowing the activation triggers beforehand helps to reduce confusion and even hesitation in moments of high stress.

Activation triggers are exactly what you might imagine. These are events or circumstances that would immediately cause the activation and deployment of your pre-established communication plan. While these events will vary from family to family and region to region, following is a short list of activation triggers that nearly everyone can start with:

- **Extended power outage:** While your time limits may be different, it's recommended that you use any power outage over twelve hours as an activation trigger. A power outage over twelve hours will likely affect local communications and will certainly require the implementation of your Communications Power Plan even if normal modes of communication are still functional.
- **Failure of cell service or Internet:** Without these services, you'll likely be immediately in an information deficit as to the cause. This will require use of backup communications to gather information and get in touch with team members who might not be in the immediate area. That could

involve not only radio communications but also rallying at pre-established rendezvous points.

- **Natural disasters:** Whether a hurricane, tornado, wildfire, and any number of other possibilities, natural disasters are notorious for causing physical damage and power outages, which are primary culprits for taking out the communication grid in that area. Even if normal communications aren't affected, preemptive measures should be taken just in case. It's always easier to activate a communication plan while normal modes of communications are still available. This way, if comms go down, your team is already set up and ready to go.
- **Civil unrest/lockdown:** Again, either of these events should be considered a preemptive activation trigger for a communication plan. These events often cause system overwhelm, which could impact comms and Internet usage for an extended period of time. If there is a civil unrest event in your vicinity, physical damage of infrastructure could soon follow.
- **News of cyberattack:** If widespread news of any kind of cyberattack is reported, events affecting communication infrastructure could soon follow. Depending on the scale and goals of the cyberattack, effects could be local, regional, national, or even global. Even if normal communications are not affected, this could be a great real-life drill for activating and testing the plan.
- **Terrorist attack:** A terrorist attack can cause physical damage, power outages, and system overwhelm, especially in the local area where the attack(s) occurs. All three of these happened simultaneously during the 9/11 terrorist attacks in 2001. Remember, it only takes one of those three consequences to impact normal communications.

Communications Tree

When activation happens, it is a good idea to have a "communications tree" in place. A communications tree is a predetermined calling/messaging protocol where one person notifies two others, then those two notify two others, and so on. It is essentially a cascading call list that reduces the overwhelm on one team member and also allows for quicker check-ins by team members. The primary communicator is typically the one who activates the plan and initiates communication through the communications tree.

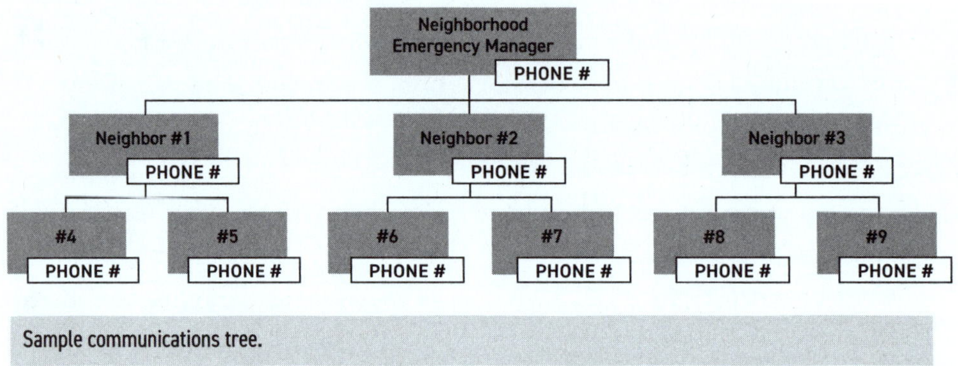

Sample communications tree.

If cell phone service is still available, a text thread can get messages out very quickly. Time is always of the essence in situations like this so a communications team text thread should be set up in advance so that time sensitive initial messaging can be sent in seconds rather than minutes.

A communications tree is especially useful when various team members are affected in various ways. Some could have cell access, others may have only radio access, others may have only Wi-Fi or Internet access. In these instances, each person in the communications tree would reference and use the various contact methods (phone/radio channel or frequency/email/social media accounts) recorded on the communication plan. If contact isn't established, then pre-established in-town or out-of-town meeting points would be used. Using this method, a team can quickly determine who is and who is not accounted for as well as their location.

Quick Action Checklist

Using the information provided in this chapter, it's now time to print the forms and complete all sections of the Family Communication Plan. Use the following quick action checklist as a visual guide for making sure all sections are completed.

❑ Family/Group Initial Emergency Communication Plan Meeting

❑ Communication Roles Assigned

- Lead communicator
- Log keeper
- Check-in coordinator
- Secondary communicator
- Runner
- Power lead
- Junior communicator

❑ Family Communication Plan

- Forms downloaded and printed from www.creekstewart.com/emergencycommunications101

❑ Local Communications Section

- Emergency contacts
- All family members
- Local fire station
- Local police
- Other: ___________________
- ICE numbers

❑ Emergency Meeting Places

- Immediate area
- In-town family meeting place
- Out-of-town meeting place

❑ Parent/Guardian Workplace Information

❑ Child School and/or Daycare Information

❑ Detailed Family Information

- ❏ Medical Contacts
- ❏ Insurance Information
- ❏ Alternate Communication Details
- ❏ Communication Kit Location
  - Primary repeater frequency/channel information
  - Second backup repeater frequency/channel information
  - Third backup repeater frequency/channel information
  - Fourth backup simplex frequency/channel information
  - Fifth backup simplex frequency/channel information
  - Established monitoring time
- ❏ Out-of-Town Communications Section
  - Out-of-town contact: 3–5 hours away
  - Out-of-town contact: 1–3 states away
- ❏ Communications Power Plan Section
  - Power Plan: Tier 1
  - Power Plan: Tier 2
  - Power Plan: Tier 3
  - Power Plan: Tier 4

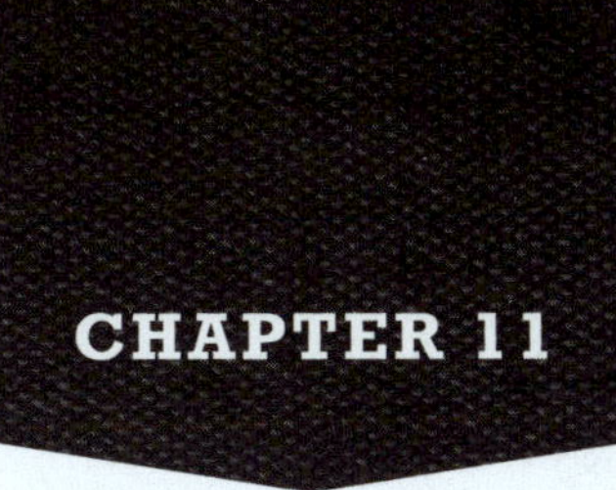

PRACTICE YOUR PLAN

In this chapter, you will learn how to develop your newfound skills through study, practice, and repetition. The development of skills is especially important with alternative communication tools such as radios, receivers, and the many details that come along with using them legally and effectively. Unfortunately, in many instances, operating these alternative communication tools are not intuitive. And in some cases, such as ham radio, you will need proper licensing, which requires an investment of time and study.

Furthermore, radio operation amongst a preparedness team or family isn't a one-person skill like fire-starting or setting up a tent. It is a skill that, in most instances, requires two people who both understand at least the basic functions and powering of the devices. And these skill requirements can vary greatly depending on the radio service and setup.

Virtually none of the tools and skills detailed throughout this book are plug-and-play. Consequently, becoming your own effective family communication manager is going to take a lot of practice, on behalf of multiple team members. In addition, like all tools, there is some routine maintenance to consider.

Licensure

The first step to practicing, legally at least, is to get your proper license(s). The vast majority of daily communication managers will choose to purchase either ham radios or GMRS radios for their backup two-way communication tools. As mentioned previously, both of these require a license. Ham radio requires that you pass an exam, GMRS does not. Regardless, before practicing on either of these radio services, follow these links to make it legal:

- Ham radio: www.fcc.gov/wireless/bureau-divisions/mobility-division/amateur-radio-service
- GMRS radio: www.fcc.gov/wireless/bureau-divisions/mobility-division/general-mobile-radio-service-gmrs

Once you have chosen your radio services and types, purchased your gear, and obtained the proper licensing, there are three main elements to mastering your skills as a radio communicator. These elements are lifestyle incorporation, routine communication drills, and regular maintenance. Let's discuss each one in detail.

Lifestyle Incorporation

The best way to master many aspects of radio and alternative communication skills is to incorporate them into your regular life. This is known as lifestyle incorporation. Using these tools in normal times helps to reduce anxiety and fear if you're ever in a position to use them in a disaster scenario. You do not want to be learning how to use a radio during a crisis!

Here are just a few simple ideas for incorporating the use of two-way radios and receivers into your everyday life:

- When someone goes to the grocery store, take a two-way radio and see how far they can communicate clearly with those back at home. Talk back and forth while in the grocery store if possible.

- Take a radio outside while doing yard work and use it to communicate with those inside the house.
- Take radios to events, such as baseball games, camping trips, or theme parks, and use them for communication.
- Have the parents or guardians take radios to work and see if they can communicate with other family members at home.

During this routine practice, make notes as to which channels or frequencies have a lot of activity and which ones are more private and may make good primary and secondary family communication frequencies/channels. Not only will this regular use help to grow skill sets for sending and receiving messages, but it will familiarize each user with how to charge the devices, change their batteries, control volume, and even estimate battery life. It will also, especially in the case of shorter-distance radios such as GMRS, give you a clear map of where your radios do and do not work. These areas of reception or dead zones can be noted on your Family Communication Plan documents in the event of a crisis.

Routine Drills

Even though practice will foster familiarity and comfort using the tools, real situation learning comes from routine drills. When it comes to communication, it's important to build a level of proficiency that directly relates to the circumstances you might experience in a real-life disaster. The only real way to do this is to practice routine drills. For communications, these drills should revolve around different aspects of your Family Communication Plan that you completed in Chapter 10. In my experience, especially for children, routine communication drills are very fun exercises. They often involve improvisation, problem-solving, the use of handheld radios, and what feels like a human scavenger hunt to communicate with and locate other family members. While there are countless drills that can be developed, following are three versions that each help to train and develop comfort in various areas of a communication plan.

HOUSE DISASTER DRILL

Description: The family is made aware that at some point during the day, a mock disaster will strike the home, forcing immediate evacuation. The disaster is marked by a certain sound, such as an air horn, bell, or beating of pans. The goal of this drill is to simulate a sudden emergency scenario during "normal life" conditions. A great way to mix up this drill is to initiate it during different times of the day, such as early morning, during meals, or just before bed. Try to focus on reinforcing the different role responsibilities that have been assigned to team members.

Action: Family members should evacuate to the immediate evacuation location assigned in the Family Communication Plan.

Lessons: This drill reinforces familiarity with the immediate evacuation location.

SCATTER DRILL

Description: The family is made aware that at some point during the day, a mock disaster will strike their area while the family is split up in two locations across town. This scenario mimics a situation when the family is separated at the onset of a disaster. This drill works best when there are two parents or guardians, and when the family or group is split up during errands or after-school activities. Each family group should have a copy of the communication plan. A good way to mix up this drill is to have a friend pretend to provide either weather-related information or first responder information that the group can use to alter and formulate plans. This may include road closures or disaster updates.

Action: A text is sent to all applicable cell phones with the following details:

Disaster Strike

All cell phone communication has been disabled

All routes to home are blocked

Must locate family members

Lessons: This drill requires the family units to meet at the pre-established in-town meeting place. To make this drill more fun and engaging, equip all members with handheld or mobile radios to practice radio communications and tuning into designated frequencies or channels.

BUG OUT LUNCH

Description: On a lazy Saturday or Sunday afternoon, the family is made aware of a sudden mock disaster scenario that requires immediate evacuation; all bug out bags and communication kits should be loaded into the car and taken to a park several miles away. The goal of this drill is situational awareness while gathering as much intel as possible. To make this drill more difficult, activate it during inclement weather such as rain, snow, or summer heat. Other items from disaster kits can be deployed as necessary.

Action: In route to the park, use any receivers such as radios, police scanners, or NOAA Weather Radios to receive inbound messages. Pretend you are listening to disaster-related messaging and gather as much information as you can about the things happening in your local area. Use a physical map or one of the previously downloaded navigation cell phone apps for navigation to the park. Once you arrive at the park, fix a family lunch from the bug out bags while listening to inbound messages on radios and receivers and continue to gather information about the things happening in your local area. Use radios to scan frequencies and channels and to pick up information from other conversations.

Lessons: This drill focuses on developing familiarity with receiving inbound messages and alerts outside of the home and using those messages to paint a picture of what is happening around you.

DISASTER MARCO POLO

Description: This drill can be done either in a large indoor mall, a downtown city location, or in vehicles. The family group should be split into two units, each preferably with a parent or guardian. Each unit should have a handheld radio. Finding each other in this scenario requires problem-solving, clues, and triangulation rather than GPS tracking. This drill promotes situational awareness in busy areas and directional skills.

Action: A starting point (ground zero) is established. Each unit has 15 minutes to spread out and hide before the game begins. The game is simple. When one unit sends the message MARCO, the other unit must reply with the name of a nearby business or sign. Generic names such as STOP or TURN RIGHT cannot be used. They must be specific names that can be used by the other unit as a clue to the location, such as "Barker Street" or "Burger King." If communications are compromised by distance, then each unit must move closer to ground zero until comms are re-established. The first unit to spot the other wins the game.

Lessons: This drill focuses on the quick back and forth use of handheld radios while on the move. It also familiarizes each family member with the distance capability of radios in various environments.

These are just four of countless fun and engaging drills that can be developed and practiced to increase familiarity and learn skills. The use of Family Communication Plan documents, various radios, and receivers during these fun drills will go a long way to reducing stress and anxiety in the midst of a real-life crisis.

DESIGNING YOUR OWN DRILLS

After practicing a few of these drills, you and your team will likely have many ideas for other fun drills. Designing your own drills is a lot of fun and can add much needed variety to regular practice. Following is a list of items to consider when custom-tailoring a communication drill for your family, team, or group. You can use this list as a template for quickly outlining new drill ideas.

- Drill Name:
- Type (Evacuation/Recon/Check-In/Receiving Messages):
- Location:
- Goal of Drill:
- Tools Used:
- Who Participates:
- Success Criteria:
- What We Learned:
- Areas for Improvement:

COMMUNICATION EXERCISES (COMEX)

A COMEX is a thorough and in-depth communication drill. The concept of a COMEX originated in the military communication circles, but any communications team will benefit from regularly scheduled COMEXs. A good COMEX simulates real-world, bad-day scenarios and will test, stress, and validate a communication plan, team, and system.

How to Plan and Conduct Your Own COMEX

- **Concept:** Design a scenario that represents a likely event for your geographic area, environment, or social/political climate.
  - Recreate historical events (for example, a tornado or earthquake that has occurred in the past).
  - Reimagine a scenario of a likely future event drawn from current events.
- **Conditions:** Establish the scope of operation and mission area.
  - A COMEX works best when multiple families, groups, or organizations work together but only involve those with shared interests or purposes.
  - Identify the geographic boundaries.
  - List operational limits.
- **Personnel:** Establish roles and responsibilities.
  - Leadership.
  - Participants.
  - Observers.
  - Evaluators.
  - Teams.
  - Individuals can have multiple roles, and a single role might be shared by a few individuals.
- **Objectives and Tasks:** Outline measurable objectives and define parameters of operation.
  - Identify objectives.
  - Assign measurable tasks to be accomplished by individuals and teams.
  - Set limits for what methods, gear, and technology may be used to accomplish the tasks.
  - Introduce unannounced conditions, obstacles, and problems (surprises and curveballs) during the COMEX.

- **Schedule:** Schedule a date or dates.
  - A COMEX can last hours, days, or weeks to reflect the scenario.
  - "Time compressing" long periods of inactivity can help prevent boredom.
  - Avoid dates that might limit participation.
  - Establish a start (STARTEX) and end (ENDEX).
- **Operations Order (OPORD):** Create an OPORD that lists the previous information.
  - Share the OPORD with all stakeholders and participants.

Here's a sample COMEX OPORD:

- **Concept**
  - A squall line has passed through the county.
  - High winds, tornadoes, and heavy rain have rendered all phone, cell, and Internet service inoperable.
  - Electricity is out in more populous areas, leading to sporadic looting.
  - Net control will activate nets on the ham and GMRS repeaters listed in the group's comms plan.
- **Conditions**
  - Internet, cell, and landline use is forbidden.
  - Ham, GMRS, and FRS radios are approved.
  - Facilities and gear will be powered by a backup source only (generator, battery, solar).
  - No main power is permitted and medical equipment is exempt.
  - All reports will reflect actual conditions.
  - Procedures will be followed per the group's comms plan.
- **Personnel**
  - Net Control: Joe (W1WCN/WSGU948).
  - Participants: All family members ages eight and older.
  - Observers: Darren, Scott (KK4ECR).
  - Evaluators: Joe, Darren, and Scott.
  - Teams: Individual families will act as teams.
  - Tactical call signs are assigned per the group's comms plan.

- **Objectives and Tasks**
  - Assess the group's ability to coordinate infrastructure status reports.
    - Teams will process status reports per requests from net control.
    - Reports will be submitted by voice or digitally (MT63) using the format outlined in the group's comms plan. Status reports include, but are not limited to: Road conditions, weather observations, fuel availability, and WWV/WWVH shortwave propagation.
    - Teams should be prepared to monitor frequencies for the entire duration of the COMEX (overnight).
  - Assessments:
    - Ability to operate continuously for 24 hours or more.
    - Voice procedures.
    - Digital capabilities.
- **Schedule**
  - STARTEX: 8:00 PM, Friday, April 4, 2025.
  - ENDEX: 10:00 PM, Saturday, April 5, 2025.
  - This COMEX will take place in one (1) phase.
  - Team After Action Reports are due within 10 days of ENDEX.

A COMEX provides an excellent opportunity to do a deep dive into procedures, protocols, and practices. But it can also be a lot of fun. For example, in the previous sample COMEX, younger participants enjoy parent-sanctioned staying up late to monitor the family's radio.

Here are some kid-friendly status reports children can prepare for and communicate on the radio:

- Measure the depth of snow in inches and then convert to metric before transmitting.
- Report the type of clouds (stratus, cumulus, and so on) at a particular time.
- Record and report the number of planes that pass overhead during a specific period.
- Measure, average, and report the body temperature of all family members.
- Monitor the frequency and note each time someone doesn't follow radio protocol in the communication plan. (This one will truly test how well the

adults operate. Trust us, the little ones *will* notice the details. This author learned this lesson the hard way.) For example:

- Forgets to use a pro word when appropriate.
- Uses the wrong phonetic letter.
- Neglects to identify a station properly.

Assessments, Hot Washes, and After Action Reports

Communication plans and strategies are only as good as the lessons learned through practice, drills, and simulated emergency tests (SETs). Drills and SETs are beneficial only with an intentional assessment process, often called a hot wash. Practicing a drill without identifying what worked and what didn't and using that information to improve the plan is just a role-playing game.

A hot wash is an informal discussion soon after a real-life disaster or event. It should include all participants. It's most valuable in an atmosphere that encourages input from everyone in attendance. (The term "hot wash" originated in the military to describe a candid conversation that took place while combatants cleaned their weapons immediately after an incident.)

There are four domains or areas to explore in a hot wash. This is sometimes referred to as the SWOT assessment.

- Strengths
- Weaknesses
- Opportunities
- Threats

Here are some questions to ask in a hot wash:

- What did we expect?
- Did the expected happen? Why or why not?
- What worked? Why?
- What didn't work? Why?
- What was missing?
- What wasn't needed?

- Who didn't feel part of the team?
- What would everyone like a second chance at?
- What was one thing or new skill that each individual learned?
- Did everyone feel properly equipped for their role?

It's good for everyone to keep personal notes during the meeting. Following the meeting, each participant should create a personal After Action Report (AAR) based on their perceptions of the event and hot wash. Keep the personal AARs short and sweet—four paragraphs of three or four sentences each.

- Positives
- Negatives
- What to keep
- What to discard

The personal AARs will then be consolidated into a single team AAR that can be used to make improvements, edits, and adjustments to the overall communication plan.

Regular Maintenance

Skill and familiarity is useless with gear and software that has become damaged, out-of-date, or compromised in some unforeseen way. Routine maintenance of tools and software updates are required duties of any dedicated family communication manager. This includes three main categories: physical maintenance, software/technology updates, and damage prevention.

PHYSICAL MAINTENANCE

All electronic devices are subject to various issues. Before delving into a list of routine maintenance items, it's important to note that storage conditions play a large role in preventing and prolonging physical damage. All your communication tools should be stored in an area that meets the following conditions:

- **Dry:** Storage location should always be dry as any moisture will be detrimental to all parts of radio tools.

- **Free from temperature extremes:** Avoid storing in areas with extreme temperature swings or prolonged exposure to extreme temperatures. This reduces the possibility of internal condensation. Steady room temperature is preferred.

In addition to the two previous conditions, it is highly recommended that all communication tools be stored in a convenient place for easy access in the event that a sudden evacuation is required. These conditions apply to all radio accessories, chargers, and backup batteries as well.

Following are the items that should be checked periodically (at least once every three months) to assure optimum performance:

Power Maintenance

- **Battery retention:** Despite proper storage, batteries have a shelf life. Routinely check that your device batteries can take and hold a charge.
- **Corrosion:** Batteries are also prone to corrosion. Inspect and clean battery contact points on both the battery and inside the device.
- **Battery age:** Some manufacturers list expiration dates in their rechargeable battery packs. Replace these when instructed to do so.

Antenna Maintenance

- Use binoculars or drone to inspect antennas that are out of reach.
- Check all antennas for cracks, bends, or broken connections.
- Detach removable antennas and clean contact points with a clean, dry cloth; check for corrosion and apply sealant if necessary.
- Check mounting hardware for rust or corrosion; retighten loose fittings.

Device Component Checks

- **Push-to-talk button:** Check that the PTT button on your radios isn't sticking or jammed in any way.
- **Keypad buttons:** Check that all keypad buttons are in working order.
- **Other components:** Check for corrosion on or buildup on speakers, microphones, charging ports, and accessory ports.

Seams and Seals

- Check to make sure all rubber seals and gaskets around the battery door or any other openings are not degraded or cracked. Super Lube brand synthetic silicone grease is a good choice to keep these rubber seals and gaskets lubricated.

Accessory Checks

- **Chargers and cords:** Check to make sure all battery chargers are working properly and there are no splits or frays in charging cables.
- **Headsets:** If using earbuds or headsets with your radios or receivers, make sure these are in proper working order.

SOFTWARE/TECHNOLOGY UPDATES

Despite proper physical maintenance, many radios, devices, accessories, and apps utilize software that needs to be updated in order to work properly. This is best done in times of ideal connectivity and should be a part of your routine maintenance schedule. Following are some items to consider:

- **Offline cell phone apps:** Many of the disaster-related cell phone apps mentioned previously, such as downloadable navigation apps, require routine upgrades to operate. Take time to update these while doing your quarterly physical maintenance checks.
- **Firmware updates:** Some devices, such as cell phones and satellite phones, require routine firmware updates to maintain optimum functionality.
- **Software updates:** If using radios in unison with a PC, the related software that allows for connectivity will require routine updates. Be sure to do this in times of optimum connectivity.

DAMAGE PREVENTION

Besides the storage conditions previously mentioned, there is one other scenario that should be considered. Because radios and receivers are electronic, they are susceptible to damage from what is known as an electromagnetic pulse (EMP). An EMP is a burst of electromagnetic energy that can damage electronics. The most common causes of EMPs are nuclear weapons, solar flares, and even smaller events such as lightning strikes and power surges. This sudden burst

Improvised Faraday cage using a metal bucket (with lid) that is lined on the inside with cardboard.

of energy can fry sensitive electronic parts and circuits within devices such as radios (and even cars).

In the event of an EMP, there is an inexpensive way to protect your gear. It's called a Faraday cage, and it was invented by scientist Michael Faraday. The concept is simple. Electronic devices can be stored inside an insulated metal enclosure. This enclosure can be solid, like an ammo can, or even metal mesh, with holes throughout. It works by redirecting and dissipating the electromagnetic charge through the metal cage and around the devices. The cage can be lined with a nonconductive material like cardboard to prevent the charge from touching the devices. See the photo and caption here.

Expanding Your Team

With a clear path for practicing your plan, you'll likely grow to a point where you'll want to include extended family members, friends, church members, coworkers, and neighbors into your communications team. Let's discuss some good strategies for making this process easy and efficient.

- **Host a comms party:** A small get-together is the perfect way to show off some of your newly learned skills and acquired gear to trusted friends. A combination of teaching some basic emergency communication skills and demonstrating how some of your communication tools work is a great way to introduce someone new to the idea of backup communications.
- **Share your Family Communication Plan:** When you complete it, the physical copy of your Family Communication Plan will be very impressive,

especially to someone who doesn't have one. This is a great way to get someone interested in the idea of backup communications. Seeing your plan on paper will be very inspiring and could easily be the catalyst for action.

- **Involve them in group drills:** Consider inviting this extended network of friends to participate in a group drill with you and your family or team. This makes for a unique experience and is a crash course in how effective backup communication tools can be when paired with a solid and well-thought-out plan. Not being allowed to use cell phones is a very eye-opening experience for all people.

TRAINING NEW TEAM MEMBERS

While the aforementioned strategies are great for helping to familiarize potential team members with the idea of backup communications, consider setting up a training process and documents for when it comes to expanding your team and adding members to your communications circle. Even very simple procedures and radio operation documents can help to get new members up to speed fast—especially if you're adding new members in the middle of a crisis and they have no previous experience. Following is an outline for a basic new member training packet. You can use some or all of these criteria when creating your own.

"Quick Start" Guide for Basic Radio Operation

- How to turn on the radio
- Push-to-talk features
- How to change channels/frequencies
- How to charge the radio
- Basic radio etiquette (see Chapter 6)

Call Sign and Communicator List

- Preassigned call sign
- Communicator role and description
- List of communicators in group along with their call signs

Daily Use and Check-In Protocol

- Specific group daily use rules
- Daily or hourly check-in schedule
- Any specific communication code or language

Communications Checklist for Keeping Equipment Together

- Headset
- Chargers and cables
- Laminated documents
- Extra batteries
- Power supply/source
- Radio or device model

Tips for Engaging and Including Kids

As this chapter comes to a close, it's relevant to offer some best practices and reminders for how to engage and include children in your emergency communication plan. Including kids early on not only builds confidence but also helps fight fear. This is so important if an actual event occurs. Engagement during meetings and practice drills also prepares children to react independently if ever put in the position to do so. They will know what to do even if you're not present. Time spent working in communication drills is also nice quality time that promotes learning and interaction versus time in front of screens. Children are capable of much more than many people in modern society give them credit for. They are fast learners, good teachers, and can handle responsibility. Following are some simple ideas (and some reminders) for how to improve engagement:

- As mentioned, let kids choose their own call signs for FRS walkie-talkies. Call signs promote ownership of skills and gear.
- Assign them a role, such as junior communicator, with real responsibilities.
- Let them design and lead their own communication drill such as Radio Hide-and-Seek or a modern version of the whisper game Telephone except using radios. (To play Radio Hide-and-Seek: The child that is "it" remains

in a central location with a radio. Other children go to separate rooms throughout the house with their radios. "It" calls to them individually on the radio and asks "yes-or-no" questions about the room. "It" tries to guess what room the other child is in.)

- Create pop quizzes for radio skills and knowledge. This gives children an opportunity to show off what they've learned and practiced.
- Practice radio etiquette on and off the radios. Focus on short, clear messages, and use radio lingo such as pro words and discretionary language.
- Consider rewards such as stickers, badges, or certification cards as kids show competence in certain skills or memorize items within the communication plan.

Each of the categories in this chapter all have direct benefits to an overall communication plan, but they also have indirect benefits. Each of them increases familiarity and ultimately reduces anxiety for both adults and children in the event of a real-life crisis.

Quick Action Checklist

Using the information provided in this chapter, now it's time to make some decisions about how you'll incorporate radio communications in your lifestyle, what drill you will run, and what maintenance checks you'll build into your schedule. Use the following quick action checklist to identify which of these areas you will choose to focus on in the coming weeks and months.

Licensure: Which of these licenses do you need to obtain?

❑ Ham radio license

❑ GMRS license

Lifestyle Incorporation: List several ways you will incorporate using radio and/or receivers into your lifestyle.

❑ Taking radios to work

❑ Taking radios to grocery stores or while running errands

- ❑ Taking radios to events, parks, or theme parks
- ❑ Using radios while outside walking, doing yard work, etc.
- ❑ ____________________
- ❑ ____________________
- ❑ ____________________

Routine Drills: Which of the following drills will you run in the coming weeks?

- ❑ House disaster drill
- ❑ Scatter drill
- ❑ Bug out lunch
- ❑ Disaster Marco Polo
- ❑ ____________________
- ❑ ____________________
- ❑ ____________________

Regular Maintenance: Identify the maintenance checks you'll work on in the coming weeks or use the following list as a checklist during routine maintenance checks.

- ❑ Storage area choice and development
    - Dry
    - Free from extreme temperature changes
- ❑ Physical maintenance
- ❑ Power maintenance
- ❑ Antenna maintenance
- ❑ Device component checks
- ❑ Seams and seals
- ❑ Accessory checks

- ❏ Software/technology updates
- ❏ Offline cell phone apps
- ❏ Firmware updates
- ❏ Software updates
- ❏ Damage prevention
- ❏ Faraday cage
- ❏ Expand your team
- ❏ Intentional efforts to engage and include children

CHAPTER 12

HOW TO KEEP CALM DURING AN EMERGENCY

There is nothing like a disaster to stir fear, incite panic, and expose vulnerabilities and insecurities. This has much to do with the disruption of the normal. The less normal a situation seems, the more uncertainty surfaces and the more chaotic things feel. The previous chapters have provided the knowledge, tools, and resources for you to establish a sense of normalcy when traditional modes of communication have been disrupted. The good news is that these methods and tools have been proven effective through historical events all over the world. Communicating during a crisis is possible.

This chapter will explore an equally important aspect of disaster communication—keeping calm in the midst of chaos. From having a plan and staying grounded to combat breathing and a 90-second rule, you'll learn several easy and effective strategies for staying focused when everything around you is going sideways.

The Emotional Toll of Communication Breakdowns

Our society is more connected now than ever before in human history. We receive and send a mind-boggling number of communication messages each and every day. The sudden loss of that aspect of our lives can have crippling consequences, mentally and emotionally. The truth is that we are more vulnerable than ever before, emotionally at least, to any deviation from "normal" when it comes to feeling connected.

A wide variety of responses can surface. These can range from fear and panic to withdrawal and isolation. And, history shows us that, especially with children, the emotional toll of a disaster can linger long after the disaster is over. Disasters can cause post-traumatic stress that lasts for years and even decades. Let's explore some strategies that you can combine with your Family Communication Plan to further reduce the negative emotional effects of a disaster.

Have a Plan

One of the biggest factors in reducing stress and fear during times of crisis is simply having a plan. For communications at least, this book outlines that plan. You simply have to use the information presented to make the best choices for your circumstances, budget, and goals. The quick action checklists at the end of each chapter will guide you through much of this process.

Once your custom plan is assembled, the suggested lifestyle integration ideas, routine drills, and maintenance checks will help to build proficiency in using the equipment and executing the plan. When combined with required study and licensure, you'll feel like a competent family communication manager in no time flat.

Developing your Family Communication Plan requires you to make important decisions about where to go and how to communicate before a crisis happens. Making sound and rational decisions in the midst of a crisis is very difficult. Your Family Communication Plan provides all the answers. Your job during a disaster is simply to execute a pre-established plan. Beyond a plan, however, there are several strategies for staying calm in stressful situations that are worth outlining.

Staying Grounded in the Chaos

Following are several techniques that you can use during a crisis to reduce anxiety and regain focus on executing your communication plan.

COMBAT BREATHING

Breathing, and the control of it, has a powerful effect on the human psyche. There is a technique used by military and first responders that is very effective for helping to manage stress in the midst of chaos. It's called combat breathing. Here are the four steps to use it:

1. Start by breathing in while counting: 1, 2, 3, 4.
2. Then, stop and hold your breath while counting: 1, 2, 3, 4.
3. Finally, exhale while counting: 1, 2, 3, 4.
4. Repeat steps 1, 2, and 3 until you calm down and begin to think more clearly.

This methodical controlled breathing can have dramatic effects on regaining focus and helping to prevent being overcome by anxiety.

GROUNDING

Grounding is the use of a variety of techniques that help you to focus your senses on the present moment. This includes what you can see, touch, hear, taste, and smell. When combined with the combat breathing technique, it can have powerful results. The basis of grounding is focusing on something besides fear and anxiety. Focus can help shut out negative feelings. Here are several specific grounding techniques:

- **Smell:** What do you smell? Focus on the scents around you and try to identify where they are coming from. Think about moments when you've smelled them before or memories that are related to them. Are there multiple scents? What are they?
- **Touch:** Pick up something nearby. Focus on what it feels like: texture, temperature, material, weight, and so on. What color is it? Is it new, old, human-made, or natural? Where did it come from?
- **Taste:** Eat something and focus on the experience of tasting it. What does it taste like? What is the texture? Is it dry or moist, hot or cold, soft or hard? When was the last time you tasted this thing? Where did it come from? How does the taste make you feel?

- **Sound:** What sounds do you hear? Dogs, birds, water, wind, television, people? How many different sounds do you hear? Are they loud or soft? Are they close or far away? What is making these sounds? Do you like any of them?
- **Sight:** What do you see around you? Find something that makes you happy, like a photo. Where did this item come from? What memories does it bring to mind? Is it new, old, made, bought, or a gift? How much did it cost? How does it make you feel? Focus on all of the thoughts that come to mind when you look at this item and all the memories that come with it.

THE 90-SECOND RULE

According to neuroscientist Jill Bolte Taylor, "When a person has a reaction to something in their environment, there's a 90-second chemical process that happens in the body; after that, any remaining emotional response is just the person choosing to stay in that emotional loop."

It's impossible to be fully human and avoid something *setting us off*. We display a negative response because something caught us off guard. This is particularly true under the stress of a disaster or emergency.

According to Taylor's 90-second rule, " . . . the moment you have the thought that there's a threat and that circuit of fear gets triggered, it will stimulate the emotional circuitry related to it, which is the fight-or-flight reaction. That will trigger a physiological dumpage of usually norepinephrine or anger into the bloodstream. It will flush through you and flush out of you in less than 90 seconds. So from the moment you think the thought that triggers that whole cascade of events to the chemical flushing out of you takes less than 90 seconds."

But why does the negative response linger? Why do you stay "triggered" in a state of fear after the threat has passed or wallow in a lousy mood longer after the offense has passed? Whenever the memory or recounting of the negative stimulus catches you off guard, your body re-releases the chemicals that need to be flushed out, and the 90-second timer starts again.

So how do you stop the cycle? (What follows is the authors' approach, not Dr. Taylor's.)

1. Do your best to recognize the feeling for what it is, a feeling that sucks at the moment but will pass. Combat breathing and grounding techniques are excellent techniques to "keep your head" while the chemicals flush out.
2. Concentrate on the feelings, not the stimulus, or as this author likes to say, "Dance with the fear you've been running from." Recounting or dwelling on the original trigger re-stimulates the negative emotions and restarts the 90 seconds it takes to flush them.
3. Direct your thoughts to your physiological response. Notice your breath and heart rate. Are your teeth clenched? Do you have tunnel vision, ringing in your ears, or tingling on your skin? Do your best not to judge the sensations; just identify them.
4. Avoid intentionally suppressing or trying to forget the experience. Doing so re-triggers the response. Focusing on your reaction rather than the catalyst puts the trigger in its place. You recognize that the event happened, but it's not your responsibility. How you respond is your responsibility.
5. If possible, go outside. Being immersed in nature significantly reduces the chances of re-triggering a negative response. Counter-intuitively, the lack of order in nature has a calming effect on us. This is why nobody has ever said, "I'm stepping inside to calm down." No, everyone goes outside for a "breath of fresh air" to calm down. While outside, identify natural objects in the environment with what you feel physiologically. For example, a nearby stream might represent the norepinephrine flushing from our brains. A gentle breeze is our breath, and the rustling leaves of a tree are the tingling in our fingers. The point is to externally observe our physiological response while still being in touch with it. If it's not possible to go outside, focus on something natural inside, such as a plant, sleeping pet, fish tank, and so on.
6. Journal your observations. Recording the experience helps you dispassionately assess what occurred and prepare for the inevitable future event.

Successfully applying the 90-second rule takes practice; it's like a muscle that needs to be exercised to strengthen it. Apply it to the little stressors of everyday life, such as snarled traffic, rude interactions, incorrect drive-thru orders, and so on. You might not see when the big crisis comes, but your response won't catch you off guard.

Using Your Communication Tools to Reduce Anxiety

Not only can having a plan help to reduce anxiety, but how you use the communication tools included in that plan can help even more. Following are several specific tips for how to use your communication tools in the midst of chaos to help reduce anxiety.

- **Seek credible information:** Conspiracy theories on all political sides abound during many disasters. Avoid listening to radio frequencies or channels that push divisive narratives and messaging. Instead, focus on inputs from people and organizations that are credible.
- **Use appropriate channels:** Avoid channels that have nothing to do with solutions or messaging related to your current situation.
- **Make meaningful connections:** Use your communication tools to build meaningful relationships with people inside and out of the disaster zone.
- **Be positive:** Be positive in all communications. Negativity solves no problems.
- **Be watchful:** Use your communication tools to become watchful and informed. This can include the use of local scanners and NOAA Weather Radios to receive a wide range of information.
- **Protect the vulnerable:** Some disaster messaging may not be appropriate for children and can increase anxiety. Be intentional and thoughtful when it comes to this and protect them from negative, emotional, or explicit messaging.

How a communication manager conducts themselves plays a huge role in the stress levels of their team. For example, read the following two messages. Which one do you think best reduces anxiety, Message 1 or Message 2?

1. Message 1: "I hope you guys can hear me. The roads are horrible and I have no idea if we can even make it under these conditions. I'm trying to get to the pharmacy where we're supposed to meet but just don't know . . . Can anyone hear me??"
2. Message 2: "Hamilton 2, this is Hamilton 1, I'm in route to the primary in-town checkpoint. Having to travel slow. ETA 30 minutes. All is well. Over."

Message 2, of course, is calm, professional, and reduces anxiety rather than promoting it. Shortness combined with brevity produces a sense of calm despite the circumstances. Panicked communications do no one any good.

Teaching Children to Stay Calm

Many people who are preparing for emergency communications have children. Children take their emotional cues from parents and guardians and must be given special consideration when it comes to emergency communications. It is of utmost importance to include children in your training exercises and regular use of equipment so that they too build familiarity and confidence with backup communication concepts.

One great way to do this is to give children a special role with a call sign and responsibilities. Let them help choose their call sign. Creek's CB call sign when he was a little boy was TADPOLE and it is still a fond memory to this day. This role should come with a handheld walkie-talkie. An inexpensive FRS radio or even a GMRS radio are great options that will allow them to participate hands-on. Their responsibilities could be to help listen to the NOAA radio or even to charge devices. Even simple responsibilities can help a child feel a part of a team.

One of the most important things you can do to help children be comfortable with emergency communications is simply to let them practice with the radios around the house. All kids like to use a walkie-talkie. When they head outside to play, send them with a walkie-talkie and encourage them to communicate what they're doing and where they are with you. Taking the radios to grocery stores, theme parks, or sporting events is also excellent real-world practice. Challenge children to use proper radio etiquette; call signs; and short, concise messages. This practice will not only make them better communicators but also more confident radio operators. Fun radio games, such as Radio Hide-and-Seek, are a great way to combine fast action to quick communications.

Children are also more than capable of doing calming exercises such as combat breathing and grounding. In fact, an easy and effective grounding game that you can play with children during times of stress in normal life is called the 5-4-3-2-1 Grounding Game. To play, simply have the child stop and list:

- 5 things they can see
- 4 things they can hear
- 3 things they can feel
- 2 things they can taste
- Recall 1 of their favorite memories

Ultimately, there is a lot you can't control in a disaster. That's why dealing with the things you can control in the proper way is so important. You may not be able to control the disaster or the information, but you can try to control your emotions and simply execute the plan.

Communication Leadership and Emotional Leadership

If you haven't already guessed it, communication managers play a much more important role than simply relaying messages. Your tone and attitude during the disaster communications process can set the stage for how other people react. Communication managers can literally be the "calm within the storm." The tone you set can cause a ripple effect throughout your family, team, or organization.

As the source of inbound and outbound messages, your style of verbal and nonverbal communication can go a long way to reduce anxiety and provide a team with the confidence and reassurance it needs to subdue panic. While you may not be able to control the information, you can control how that information is delivered. Sometimes, a calm and steady countenance is all that's required to deliver bad news in a positive way.

This concept isn't one that's often covered in textbooks about emergency communications but any person who has been through the trenches of a disaster knows how important proper leadership can be. A communication manager not only has a responsibility to execute a communication plan but also to be an emotional leader to those within their communications sphere of influence.

Communicating Electronically with Someone in Distress

As Creek likes to say, "It's not IF but WHEN." This is never truer than answering a scared or panicked person's phone or radio call for help. It will be up to you to help them regain their composure.

- Check yourself and remain calm. Start by using the abovementioned techniques to prepare for the unexpected phone or radio call.
- Lower the intensity, pace, and volume of your voice. The louder, more agitated, or panicked the caller gets, the softer, warmer, and more soothing your voice should get. Maintain a steady pace of words and avoid interrupting them to "get to the point." The point right now is to pour courage into them.
- Have someone with you listen in to write down the information you gather in the following steps. Your "assistant" should be preparing to contact first responders while you continue with the following steps.
- Introduce yourself by first name, ask for their first name, and use their name often. "Hi, I'm Joe. What's your name?" "Hi, Ellie, that's a pretty name. It sounds like you don't feel safe, Ellie."
- Use reassuring words and tone. There's a good chance that the person on the other end is alone, or they might be calling because someone in their party is injured or incapacitated. Electronic communication is, by definition, more isolating than talking face-to-face. Frequently let them know that they are not alone. Use the word "we." "We'll get through this." "We'll get the help we need."

- Acknowledge their observations. This doesn't mean you agree with them; it assures them they are being heard.
- Avoid assuming that everything they say is accurate. A good rule in a moment of fear is not to believe everything we think. That is especially true for the person on the other end of the conversation.
- Don't disagree with their feelings, either. In this moment, their perception is their reality. It's not our place to tell them, "It's not that bad" or "You wouldn't be able to talk to me if the flames were that close."
- Reword and repeat to them what you heard: "Did you say that the fire is right next to you?" or "It sounds like the wound is pretty bad."
- Gather objective information with clarifying questions: "Are the flames close enough for you to hit if you threw a baseball at them?" or "Is the hole one finger wide, two fingers wide, or three fingers wide?"
- If you ascertain that they are in imminent danger, help them find a safe place and instruct them to move to that place, away from immediate danger.
- Advise them about any required first aid, shelter construction, and so on that might be needed.
- If the danger is passed, instruct them to remain in place and wait for help.
- During the conversation, collect the following information. (Keep operational security [see Chapter 7] in mind if communicating by radio. It might not be prudent to gather specific contact and location information by radio. Use your best judgment.)
  - Callback information in case contact is lost.
  - Phone number if the contact is by phone.
  - Frequency and callback schedule if the contact is by radio.
  - Nature of the emergency.
  - What happened?
  - Number of people affected.
  - Injuries, illness, weather conditions, property destruction.
  - Location.
  - Address.
  - Landmarks.

- GPS coordinates.
    - US National Grid System or Military Grid Reference System.
    - Latitude/Longitude.
    - What3words.
- Tools, equipment, and gear on hand.
- First aid kit.
- Health histories.
- Medical alert bracelets, and so on.
- Communication equipment.

Once the issue or emergency is resolved, it's time to take care of you. Emergency dispatch work ranks among the top ten industries with the highest turnover rates. On average, one of every four emergency dispatchers leaves in less than a year. Helping someone through a crisis by phone or radio is off-the-chain stressful, even for the pros. Use the previous calming techniques mentioned in this chapter to revive and rejuvenate yourself. You owe it to yourself and your loved ones to lead them through the next crisis.

Quick Action Checklist

By having a Family Communication Plan and implementing a few basic proven strategies to help you and your team focus on executing that plan, you'll be well on your way to maintaining a sense of calm resolve in the midst of anything that humankind or Mother Nature throws your way. But even calming exercises such as combat breathing and grounding take practice. Use the following quick action checklist as a reminder to incorporate some of these activities into your daily life so they are not new in unexpected times of crisis.

Using the information provided in this chapter, make a concerted effort to incorporate some of the mentioned methods to help calm members of your family in times of stress. Identify which of these strategies to practice using in the coming weeks and months:

Methods to reduce anxiety and regain focus:

- ❑ Combat breathing
- ❑ Grounding
- ❑ Smell
- ❑ Touch
- ❑ Taste
- ❑ Sound
- ❑ Sight
- ❑ The 90-second rule

CONCLUSION

With well over fifty years of combined experience within the disaster preparedness and communications space, we can both attest to the fact that having a well-developed Family Communication Plan in place is one of the most critical components to any disaster preparedness plan. Whether you just use FRS radios in your cul-de-sac or establish yourself as a regional communication manager for organizations such as The Salvation Army, the skills and tools outlined in this book have, can, and will continue to save lives.

Emergency communication skills, tools, and plans are not just for "Doomsday preppers" and they are not just for an apocalyptic event. These are resources that have proven useful during winter storms, local power outages, and even family outings. Statistics increasingly remind us that natural disasters are more frequent and dangerous than ever before in recorded history. Despite our many advancements in communications technology, there are very real and present vulnerabilities when it comes to physical damage of infrastructure, loss of power, cyberattacks, and even system overwhelm.

A Family Communication Plan doesn't happen overnight. It's built one brick at a time. It's time for you to now start laying the bricks of your own customized plan. Each will be foundational in being able to effectively communicate with loved ones and first responders in the midst of crisis. These include but are not limited to:

- **Understanding vulnerabilities and weaknesses:** Knowing what could happen is fundamental in knowing what to do when it does. Start by studying what's already happened in your region and identify weaknesses.

- **Obtaining backup power solutions:** Storing or producing your own power is paramount when building an off-grid communication plan. Start with the less expensive Tier 1 and Tier 2 solutions such as power banks, extra batteries, and a small portable solar generator. Backup power is not optional; it is foundational.
- **Deciding which radio service(s) best fits your needs:** Two-way radios will be a part of any solid backup emergency communication plan. Ham, GMRS, and FRS all vary in cost, reach, and licensing requirements. The key is to choose the service that best fits your budget, goals, group size, and environment.
- **Deciding which types of radio setups are most practical for your goals:** An ideal starting place after choosing your ideal radio service is to purchase handheld radio setups. There will always be a need and use for handheld units. Ultimately, your radio setups will need to match your specific needs but always start small and work from there.
- **Obtaining required licenses to legally use your radios:** As you know, radio services such as ham radio and GMRS radio require licenses in order to legally transmit messages. The license for GMRS radio is a simple form and payment and also covers your entire family. The license for ham radio requires you to study for and pass an exam.
- **Choosing which receivers make sense for your circumstances:** Inbound disaster-related information can help you make life-saving decisions. These updates not only come from two-way radio communication but from receivers such as NOAA weather radios and multiband scanners. Keeping abreast of alerts, weather updates, and local first responder activity helps to draw a more complete picture of the overall situation. The more information you can receive, the better decisions you can make. Make it a goal to include passive receivers as a part of your emergency communication plan.
- **Expanding capabilities through advanced features such as upgraded antennas, connectivity, and mesh tools:** Simple antenna upgrades to handheld or mobile setups can drastically improve reach, clarity, and performance. Digital communications can be expanded to include personal computers, email, and mesh networks. In survival, these added features take your existing foundation and make it much more effective!

- **Downloading offline tools and apps:** Cloud-based resources will likely be unavailable in the midst of an emergency. This is why it's so important to consider setting up offline communication tools and apps *before* an event occurs.
- **Considering satellite communication options:** Satellite communication tools such as voice cell phones, two-way communicators, and even satellite-based Internet service are game changers to emergency communicators. However, each comes with a varying degree of commitment and cost.
- **Developing and mastering your communications knowledge and skills:** Routine drills at home with your family or team can help you gain the critical real-world skills that are necessary to emergency communications. These drills not only develop aptitude but also build familiarity, which reduces stress and anxiety in times of crisis.
- **Putting your Family Communication Plan on paper:** Physically documenting your plan makes your communication plan real. This plan becomes your executable step-by-step guide to navigating an unexpected crisis. An established plan ensures everyone knows exactly what to do, even if you are injured or unavailable.

These foundational bricks are a journey in and of themselves but while each of these bricks are interconnected, they also have value independently. The more you add, the more thorough your Family Communication Plan becomes. The key is to chip away at the parts that bring you the most peace toward your overall goals.

Remember, it's not IF but WHEN disaster will strike. If the disaster impacts your normal communication grid and you have not put forth the time, expense, and energy to establish backup communication options in advance, it will be nearly impossible to do during a crisis. The steps you take before a disaster strikes can make a big difference in the lives of you, your family, and your neighbors in the midst of a crisis. To a society that has become dependent on connectivity, the sudden loss of it can have devastating consequences.

Off-grid communication tools are literally a lifeline to medical attention, supplies, updates, direction, peace of mind, and so much more. Remember, peace of mind comes from preparation. Your Family Communication Plan will be a constant work in progress that changes with your lifestyle, family, and circumstances. Revisiting it for accuracy at least once a year is good practice.

If something in this book has helped you take action with your own Family Communication Plan, we would love to hear about it! Please consider leaving a review at the site where you purchased this book. We read all reviews and use the feedback to create new useful content to help others in their preparedness journey. Thank you for purchasing this book and for the contribution you're making to be more ready and able to help not only yourself but also others in the midst of crisis.

Both of us, Joe and Creek, invite you to visit our websites and join our email list, where we offer lots of great free information not only about emergency communications but also other preparedness topics. Visit us at CreekStewart.com and ValiantOutfitters.com.

INDEX

Note: Page numbers in parentheses indicate intermittent references.

A

B

C

F

G

H

I

K

Q

R

ABOUT THE AUTHORS

Creek Stewart is an expert survival instructor and the author of *Survival Hacks* and the bestselling Build the Perfect Bug Out series of books. Creek is the in-house and on-camera Survival Expert for The Weather Channel and hosts *Could You Survive? with Creek Stewart* on the network. Creek has been featured as a guest expert in numerous media outlets including *Today*, *Fox & Friends*, *The Doctors*, *Men's Fitness*, *Backpacker*, and *Outdoor Life*. Creek is the owner and founder of Willow Haven Outdoor Survival Training School, located in central Indiana, and APOCABOX, a bimonthly survival subscription box that ships to thousands of loyal subscribers every other month. He is the recipient of the prestigious Outstanding Eagle Scout Award, which is bestowed by the Boy Scouts of America to Eagle Scouts who have demonstrated outstanding achievement at the local, state, or national level.

Joe Bassett is the founder of Valiant Outfitters. As a backcountry guide, he's shared his passion for the wilderness with hundreds of people. He's also a ham radio operator who's helped countless others earn their ham radio license and develop emergency radio skills for disasters and survival. Joe has provided on-location radio support in eight disaster-stricken areas, including Puerto Rico following Hurricane Maria. He frequently speaks about team crisis preparation and the importance of communication in disasters. Learn more at ValiantOutfitters.com.